Fashion Designer's Handbook for
Adobe Illustrator

Fashion Designer's Handbook for
Adobe Illustrator

First Edition

MARIANNE CENTNER | FRANCES VEREKER

Blackwell
Publishing

© 2007 Marianne Centner and Frances Vereker

Published by Blackwell Publishing Ltd

Editorial offices:
Blackwell Publishing Ltd, 9600 Garsington Road, Oxford OX4 2DQ, UK
Tel: +44 (0) 1865 776868
Blackwell Publishing Professional, 2121 State Avenue, Ames, Iowa, 50014-8300, USA
Tel: +1 515 292 0140
Blackwell Publishing Asia Pty Ltd, 550 Swanston Street, Carlton, Victoria 3053, Australia
Tel: +61 (0)3 8359 1011

First edition published 2007 by Blackwell Publishing Ltd

2   2007

ISBN: 978-1-4051-6055-1

Library of Congress Cataloging-in-Publication Data
Centner, Marianne.
Fashion designer's handbook for Adobe Illustrator / Marianne Centner and Frances Vereker. --
1st ed.
p. cm.
Includes index.
ISBN-13: 978-1-4051-6055-1 (pbk. : alk. paper)
ISBN-10: 1-4051-6055-1 (pbk. : alk. paper)
1. Fashion drawing--Computer aided design. 2. Fashion design--Data processing. 3. Adobe Illustrator (Computer file) I. Vereker, Frances. II. Title.

TT509.C45 2007
677'.02202856686--dc22
2006036894

A catalogue record for this title is available from the British Library

Typeset by Marianne Centner and Frances Vereker
Printed and bound in Singapore
by Markono Print Media Pte Ltd

The publisher's policy is to use permanent paper from mills that operate a sustainable forestry policy, and which has been manufactured from pulp processed using acid-free and elementary chlorine-free practices. Furthermore, the publisher ensures that the text paper and cover board used have met acceptable environmental accreditation standards.

For further information on
Blackwell Publishing, visit our website:
www.blackwellpublishing.com

TABLE OF CONTENTS

PREFACE

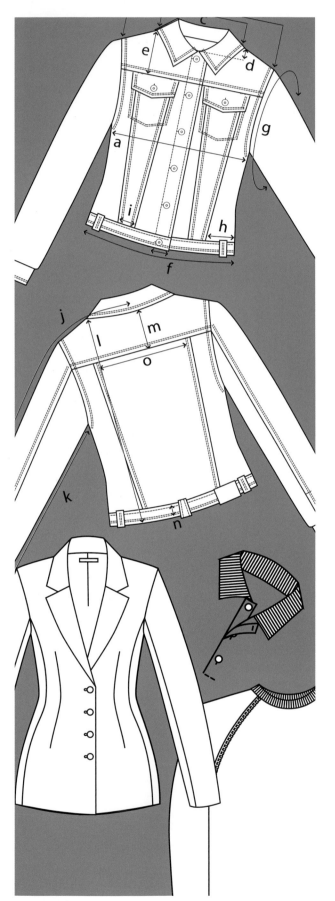

This book aims to teach Fashion Designers, both students and those in the industry, how to use **Adobe Illustrator®** to create technical drawings, fashion drawings and story boards and how to combine **Adobe Illustrator** and **Adobe Photoshop®**.

Through our own experiences of struggling with the complexities of these two vast and powerful CAD programs, we realised that it would be fantastic if the needs of the Clothing Industry were addressed. To this end we have devised an outcomes-based instruction book that will clearly and methodically take you from creating a simple shape to a fashion drawing in **Adobe Illustrator** and **Adobe Photoshop**.

Our method is a culmination of Frances Vereker's extensive experience over the past 20 years teaching fashion drawing and computer drawing to students and teachers and Marianne Centner's vast industry experience over 25 years, working exclusively in Adobe Illustrator and Adobe Photoshop for a number of years. We expect that you will have basic computer knowledge and it is with this in mind that we have adopted a step-by-step approach.

The detailed instructions are thought out in such a way as to give you as much information as you need to perform the tasks throughout the book. We do not give too much information at one time. The method we have used will easily help you grasp the concept of **Adobe Illustrator** and vector drawing. This book will be a useful and ongoing quick guide until such time as you can remember the uses of all necessary tools. Once you have grasped the basic concepts we take you through increasing degrees of complexity, introducing you to more difficult techniques.

By the time you have finished this book we expect that you will have learned all the techniques necessary to produce professional story boards and technical drawings. The final chapter of story boards will further inculcate the techniques set out in this book.

It must be understood that what we demonstrate are methods that we use, they are not the only way to achieve results - considering the vastness of both applications. We believe when you have mastered our methods you will have the confidence to allow your own creativity to lead you to the best results. We encourage you to explore and experiment as much as we do!!!

ACKNOWLEDGEMENTS

The authors gratefully acknowledge the invaluable assistance of those who have contributed to the compilation of this book. They would particularly like to thank the following:

Richard Miles (Senior Publisher) at Blackwell Publishing, who sadly passed away July 2006. On all occasions, Richard displayed a genuine caring nature to us. His emails from the other side of the world were always prompt and clear in their guidance. His commitment to our initial concept as well as his ongoing professional advice and support is gratefully acknowledged. To the team at Blackwell - Annie Choong, Shahzia Chaudhri, Madeleine Metcalfe and Andrew Hallam for their continuing advice and for making this book happen.

Lisa Walker - Professional Photographer and Christina Cauch - Fashion Model, who so generously allowed us to use their images. Mark Williams – Fashion Model and Fashion Design student, for his enthusiasm for the project and his patience in meeting our photographic needs. Also to Avril Bridges-Tull, a fashion enthusiast for further contributing to the modelling.

Efstra Dalaveris - Fashion Design and Pattern Development Lecturer, for giving up her invaluable time to assisting us in identifying our occasional inconsistencies in grammar or layout. Louise McNab for constant support and more editing. David Parker, Vinette Thompson, Justin Annesley and Joy Burk from Inki Fingus Printing for their technical advice. We would like to also thank Myer Stores Ltd and In-Time Imports Pty, Ltd. for allowing us to use some of the designs created for them by Marianne.

We would also like to thank Jurek Tanewski for even more editing and our families and friends for being so supportive during the frantic months of writing.

CHAPTER 1

THE BASICS

Drawing A Simple Shape

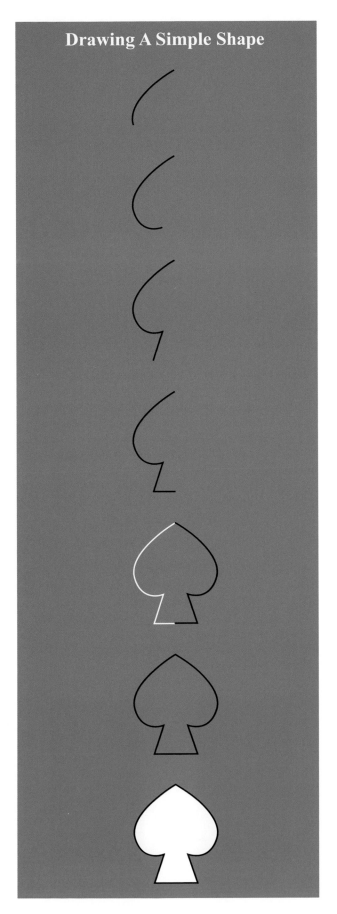

CHAPTER 1 outlines the difference between bitmap and vector images, the basics of file management and file paths, and the Adobe Illustrator tools that will be required to attain the objective of this book. There is a simple exercise at the end of this chapter.

VECTOR GRAPHICS AND BITMAP IMAGES

All computer images are either bitmap (raster) or vector images. Adobe Illustrator is a vector-based program and Adobe Photoshop is a bitmap-based program.

Vector Images:

Vector images are made of lines and curves defined by mathematical objects called vectors. A vector image is created with strokes and fills, points are joined to create lines and lines are joined to create objects. Vector graphics maintain clarity when scaled, reduced or rotated.

Scaled image

Rotated image

Actual size of vector image

All images in Adobe Illustrator are created in vector, including type. A vector graphic is resolution independent. This means it can be scaled to any size and printed on any output device. The clarity of the image is dependent on the quality of the output device. This makes vector graphics the perfect format for creating detailed technical drawings and fashion illustrations.

Bitmap Images:

Bitmap images are made up of individual pixels. Pixels are defined by a grid - the amount of pixels in an image make up the overall "dpi" of the image or the resolution of the image - 300 dpi means a resolution of 300 dots (or pixels) per inch. The higher the dpi, the higher the resolution, and subsequently the bigger the file. Most internet pictures are 72 dpi or screen resolution. Most printed images will be 300 dpi or more.

Bitmap images distort badly when they are scaled, reduced or rotated - they lose detail. Bitmap images are good for reproducing subtle gradations of colour and air brushing techniques. The final image has a softer, more realistic look than a vector image. We use bitmap images in this book to enhance story boards as well as to create realistic texture fills.

Bitmap image   Scaled bitmap image

Colour Modes or Colour Models - a colour model is any method of representing colour in graphic arts. In graphic arts and printing colours are often presented using the Pantone system. In computer graphics colours are represented in one of two modes:
RGB - Red, Green and Blue
CMYK - Cyan, Magenta, Yellow and Black

The choice of Colour Mode will depend on the end use of the graphics you are creating. If the work you are creating is going to be represented digitally - on the web or on computer or it is going to be digitally printed, you will use RGB. If the work is going to be printed on a colour plate system CMYK will be used.

HSB - Hue, Saturation and Brightness is not a colour model, but can be used when adjusting colours in RGB.

RGB is based on reflected light - the light that shines out from a monitor (computer or television). Red, blue and green are "additive" colours and when they are combined the result is white. With **RGB**, what we see represented on the screen will be closest match to what we see digitally printed.

CMYK is based on absorbed light - this is the colour model used when graphics are going to be printed on paper using a plate printing process. The medium (paper) that the colours are printed on absorb the light and when these three colours are mixed the result is black or "K".

Colours are created by mixing percentages of Cyan, Magenta and Yellow. Ideally the three colours mixed in equal proportions will create black - this is constrained by the purity of the actual ink and black is added if dark colours cannot be achieved.

When only solid colours are used in a print that consists of one or two colours Pantone Process colours are used - these are called Spot colours.

When many colours and fine gradients are required, Four-Colour Process is the preferred printing method. Colours are created by printing dots of pure colour and black adjacent to each other - our eyes then mix these colours to produce the desired effect. Photographs are usually printed with this process.

Considering that the normal method of printing in the Fashion Industry is digital, we would recommend working in **RGB** colour mode.

CREATE, SAVE AND CUSTOMISE A NEW FILE

Step 1: Opening A New File

- Click onto **File** in the menu bar
- **New** Hot Key **Ctrl N**   Apple OS **Cmd N**
- A dialogue box will appear - do not name the file
- **Artboard Setup**
- Select **Size: A4**
- **Orientation: Portrait** (▣)
- **RGB Color** (◉)
- **OK**

Step 2: Saving A New File

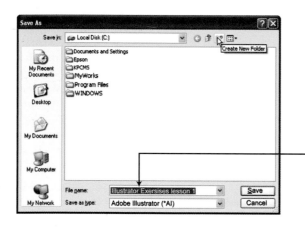

- Click onto **File**
- **Save File**
- An option box will appear
- Go to **Drive C**
- Click onto **Create New Folder** 📁 New Folder
- Name the folder 📁 Illustrator Lessons
- Click onto the new folder 📁 Illustrator Lessons
- This will open the folder
- Type the new file name in the File Name box - *Illustrator Exercises lesson 1*
- **Save** the file

  *Save the file you are working on every **10 minutes** Hot Key **Ctrl S** Apple OS **Cmd S***

Step 3: Customise The Work Area

- Click onto **Window** in the menu bar - a drop-down menu will appear
- Select the following palettes:

1. **Align**
2. **Pathfinder** will open at the same time as **Align**
3. **Color**
4. **Navigator**
5. **Swatches**
6. **Stroke**
7. **Tools**

- When a new file is opened, the program will usually default to the above palettes

- Click onto **View** in the menu bar - a drop-down menu will appear
- Select **Show Rulers** Hot Key **Ctrl R** Apple OS **Cmd R**

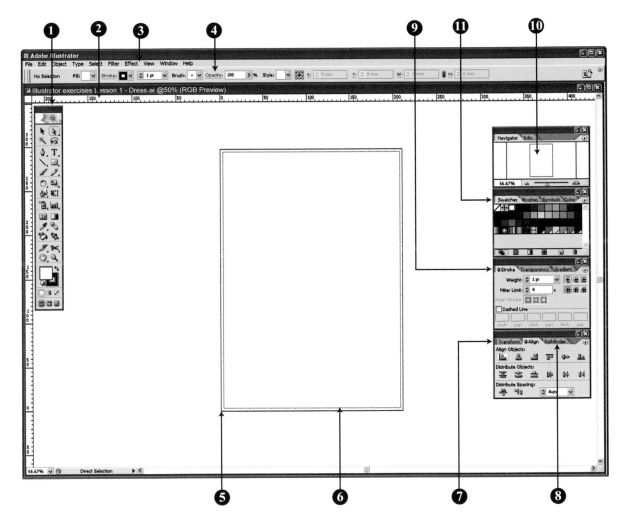

1 **Toolbox** - this contains the tools that will be used to create images

2 **Ruler -** guide lines can be pulled out from the rulers

3 **Menu Bar -** clicking onto menu items activates drop-down menus with a list of commands and sub-menus

4 **Control Palette -** this is an efficient method of accessing palettes and commands quickly

5 **Artboard -** this is the visible work area and only work within this area can be viewed in the **Navigator** palette - the **Artboard** does not need to be the same size as the paper

6 **Printable Area -** this is the area that will print out on a given paper size

7 **Align** Palette - gives you the option to align and space objects

8 **Pathfinder** Palette - allows you to cut, divide and merge shapes

9 **Stroke** Palette - gives you the option to make the stroke thicker and thinner and to choose which ends and corners you would like on your line as well as the **Dashed Line** option

10 **Navigator** Palette - allows you to navigate around the specified working area by clicking on the window and moving (a hand will appear) or by using the zoom sliding bar at the bottom of the box

11 **Swatches** Palette - provides an easy way to select and use commonly used colours, gradients and pattern swatches. You can also mix your own colours, create your own gradients and pattern swatches

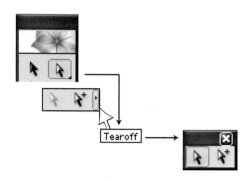

Selection Tools:

Selection Tool Hot Key **V**
Direct Selection Tool Hot Key **A**

- Click onto the black arrow at the corner to access the **Tear off** options

- The **Selection Tool** Hot Key **V** allows you to pick up and move single objects or a *group* of objects

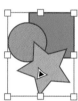

- The **Direct Selection Tool** Hot Key **A** allows you to pick up and manipulate anchor points (**a**) and handles (**b**)

- The **Group Selection Tool** allows you to pick up and move single objects from *within* a group of objects, there is no Hot Key for this tool

To deselect click away from any objects onto the work area

Click

Swap fill & Stroke
Hot Key **Shift X**

Colour
Hot Key <

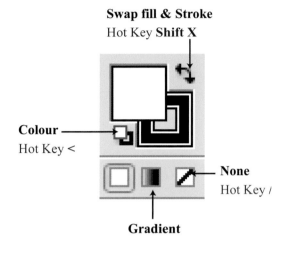

None
Hot Key /

Gradient

Fill - the solid area within a shape
Stroke - the outline around a shape

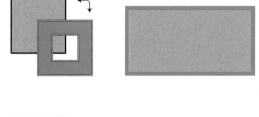

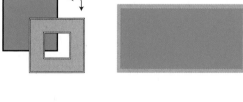

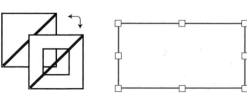

- To activate either the **Fill** or the **Stroke,** click onto the required box and that box will appear at the front
- Clicking onto a colour in the **Swatches** palette will change the colour to the new colour in the fill or the stroke

- The fill box is in front
- You can now change the fill colour

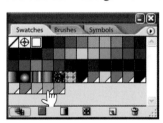

- Hot Key **X** will bring the stroke to the front
- You can now change the stroke colour

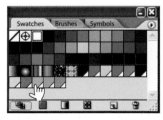

- By clicking onto the corner arrows Hot Key **Shift X** the colours in the fill and stroke boxes will swap

- By clicking onto the **None** box (▧) in the swatches box or in the tool box or Hot Key / the colour will be removed

SHAPE TOOLS

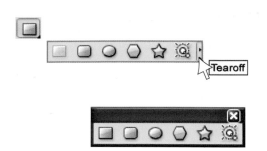

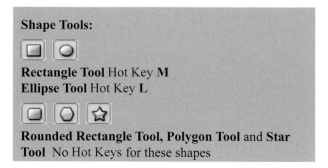

Click, shift

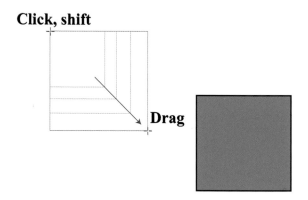

Drag

- **Tear-off** the shape options
- There are 5 different shapes - **Rectangle, Rounded Rectangle, Ellipse, Polygon** and **Star**

Drawing A Rectangle:

- Select a colour in the fill box and black in the stroke box (▣)
- Click onto the **Rectangle** Hot Key **M** in the tool box
- Click onto the work area and without releasing the mouse drag the mouse into a **Rectangle**
- Holding the **Shift** key while dragging will create a rectangle with even sides - a square

  Or:

- Click onto the **Rectangle Tool** Hot Key **M**
- *Left* mouse click onto the working area
- An option box will appear
- Type the **Width** and **Height** you require in this box
- Select **OK**

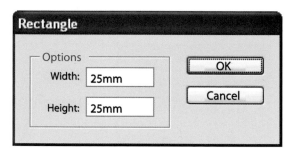

Drawing An Ellipse:

- Click onto the **Ellipse** Hot Key **L** in the tool box
- Click onto the work area and without releasing the mouse drag the mouse into an **Ellipse**
- Holding the **Shift** key while dragging will create a circle

  Or:

- Click onto the **Ellipse Tool** Hot Key **L**
- Left mouse click onto the working area
- An option box will appear
- Type the **Width** and **Height** you require in this box
- Select **OK**

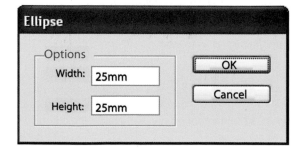

To Undo an action
*Hot Key **Ctrl Z** Apple OS **Cmd Z***
To Re-do an action
*Hot Key **Shift Ctrl Z** Apple OS **Shift Cmd Z***

Drawing A Rounded Rectangle:

- Click onto the **Rounded Rectangle Tool** in the tool box
- Click onto the work area and without releasing the mouse drag the mouse into a **Rounded Rectangle**
- Holding the **Shift** key while dragging will create a rounded rectangle with even sides - a square

Or:

- Click onto the **Rounded Rectangle Tool**
- Left mouse click onto the working area
- An option box will appear
- Type the **Width, Height** and **Corner Radius** required in this box
- Select **OK**

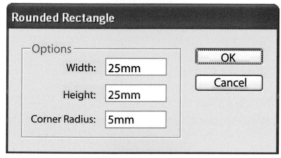

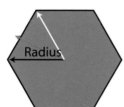

Drawing A Polygon

- Click onto the **Polygon Tool** in the tool box
- Click onto the work area and without releasing the mouse drag the mouse into a **Polygon**
- Holding the **Shift** key while dragging, keep the orientation of the polygon straight

Or:

- Click onto the **Polygon Tool**
- Left mouse click onto the working area
- An option box will appear
- Type the **Radius** and quantity of sides required in this box
- Select **OK**

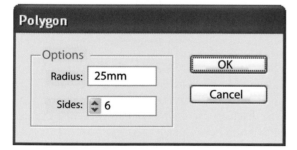

Drawing A Star:

- Click onto the **Star Tool** in the tool box
- Click onto the work area and without releasing the mouse drag the mouse into a **Star**
- Holding the **Shift** key while dragging, keep the orientation of the star straight

Or:

- Click onto the **Star Tool**
- Left mouse click onto the working area
- An option box will appear
- Type **Radius 1** and **2** and the quantity of **Points** required in this box
- Select **OK**

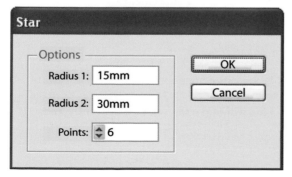

SELECT AND MOVE AN OBJECT

- Click onto the centre of a filled object or the stroke or outline of an object without fill with the **Selection Tool** Hot Key **V** to select the object

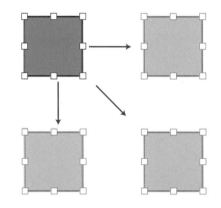

- **Move An Object:**

- Holding down the left mouse button drag the selected object

- Holding down **Shift** after selecting and starting to drag the object will move the object in a straight vertical or horizontal line or at an angle of 45°

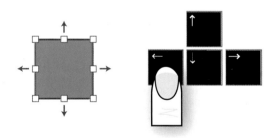

Or:

- Select object with **Selection Tool** Hot Key **V**
- Using the direction arrows on the keyboard will nudge objects left, right or up and down the distance that the **Keyboard Increment** in **Preferences** is set at

- **To Set Keyboard Increment:**

- Click onto **Edit** in the menu bar
  ↓
  Select **Preferences**
  ↓
  General
  Hot Key **Ctrl K** Apple OS **Cmd K**
  ↓
- Go to **Keyboard Increment**

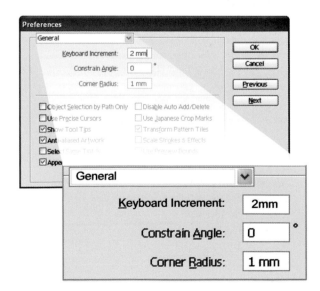

- Type measurement into the white box - **2mm**
- Select **OK**
- **This will move the selected object by 2mm**

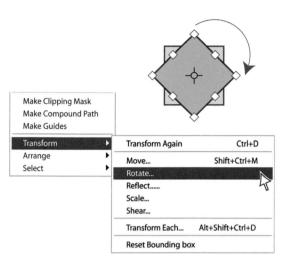

Selection Tool Hot Key **V**
Rotate Tool Hot Key **R**

- Select the object with the **Selection Tool** Hot Key **V**
- Select the **Rotate Tool** Hot Key **R**
- Holding down the left mouse button, move the mouse in the intended direction of rotation

- To rotate the object at a **90°**, **180°** or **45°** angle press the **Shift** key after you have started to drag the object

Or:

- Select the object with the **Selection Tool** Hot Key **V**
- Right click the mouse and a sub menu will appear
- Select **Transform**
- Select **Rotate**
- Type in the degree of rotation required, that is **45°**
- Select **OK**

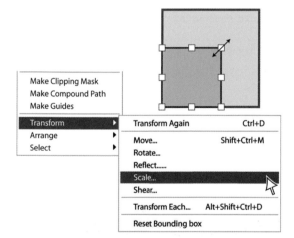

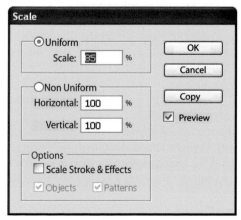

Scale An Object:

Selection Tool Hot Key **V**

- Select object with **Selection Tool** Hot Key **V**
- Place cursor at any of the anchor points ( ) of the bounding box
- An arrow (↔) will appear
- Dragging the mouse in any direction will randomly scale the object
- Holding down the **Shift** key when dragging will proportionately scale the object

Or:

- Right click the mouse
- A sub-menu will appear
- Select **Transform**
- Select **Scale**
- Type in the percentage of transformation required
- Tick (☑) the preview box to preview the action
- Select **OK**

COPY AND ROTATE COPY AN OBJECT

*grab the perimeter of the object
hold down (w/pen tool); drag; alt key
release left button*

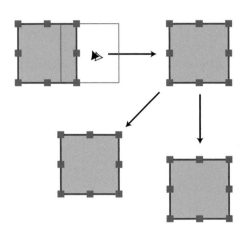

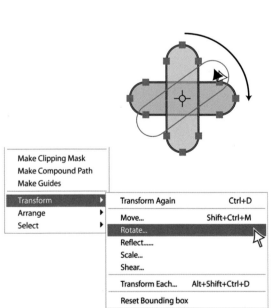

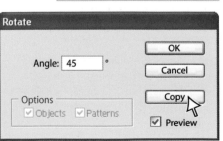

Copy An Object:

Selection Tool Hot Key **V**

- Select the object with the **Selection Tool** Hot Key **V**
- Holding down the left mouse button, start to drag the object
- Only once you have started dragging the object, press the **Alt** key and a double arrow will appear (▶)
- To copy the object in a **90°**, **180°** or **45°** angle, press the **Shift** key at the same time as the **Alt** key *after* you have started to drag the object

Or:

- Select object with the **Selection Tool** Hot Key **V**
- Copy the object
  Hot Key **Ctrl C** Apple OS **Cmd C -** to copy
  Hot Key **Ctrl F** Apple OS **Cmd F -** copies the object to the front
- Use direction arrows on keyboard to move the object left, right, up or down
- This will move the object the distance that the **Keyboard Increment** in **Preferences** is set at

Rotate Copy An Object:

Selection Tool Hot Key **V**
Rotate Tool Hot Key **R**

- Select the object with the **Selection Tool** Hot Key V
- Click onto the **Rotate Tool** Hot Key R
- Holding down the left mouse button, start to drag the object
- Only once you have started dragging the object, press the **Alt** key, a double arrow will appear (▶)
- To copy and rotate the object at a **90°**, **180°** or **45°** angle, press the **Shift** key at the same time as the **Alt** key after you have started to drag the object

Or:

- Right click the mouse
- A sub-menu will appear
- Select **Transform** ⟶ **Rotate**
- Type in the percentage of rotation required
- Click onto the **Preview** box (☑) to preview the action
- Select **Copy**

Rotate Copy An Object Continued:

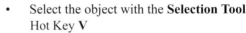

Selection Tool Hot Key **V**
Rotate Tool Hot Key **R**

- Select the object with the **Selection Tool** Hot Key **V**
- Click onto the **Rotate Tool** Hot Key **R**
- Place the cursor on the rotate axis point (-◇-), hold down the left mouse button and drag the axis to a new centre point
- Release, but *do not* deselect the object
  Holding down the left mouse button, start to drag the object
- Only once you have started dragging the object, press the **Alt** key, a double arrow will appear (▶)
- To copy and rotate the object at a **90°**, **180°** or **45°** angle, press the **Shift** key at the same time as the **Alt** key after you have started to drag the object

Press left button before selecting the object (handwritten note)

must V-R -alt-shift for every petal to copy & rotate (handwritten note)

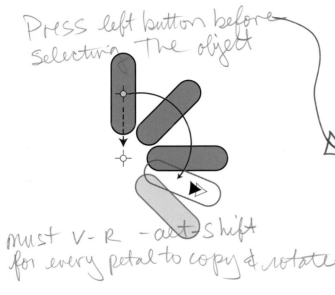

Group Objects:

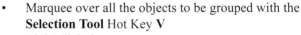

Selection Tool Hot Key **V**
Direct Selection Tool + (no Hot Key)

- Marquee over all the objects to be grouped with the **Selection Tool** Hot Key **V**
- Right click the mouse
- A sub menu will appear
- Select **Group**
- Or simply press Hot Key **Ctrl G** Apple OS **Cmd G** and the objects will be grouped together

*The objects can now be moved as one object or if part of the object needs to be moved but still remain part of the group, you can use the **Direct Selection Tool +***

- Conversely, to **Ungroup** the objects
- Select the grouped object with the **Selection Tool** Hot Key **V**
- Right click the mouse, a sub menu will appear
- Select **Ungroup** or simply press Hot Key **Shift Ctrl G** Apple OS **Shift Cmd G** and the objects will be ungrouped

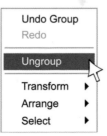

Arranging The Layer Order Of Objects:

Rectangle Tool Hot Key **M**
Ellipse Tool Hot Key **L**
Star Tool no Hot Key
Selection Tool Hot Key **V**

| Undo Typing |
| Redo |
| Group |
| Join |
| Average... |
| Make Clipping Mask |
| Make Compound Path |
| Make Guides |
| Transform ▶ |
| **Arrange ▶** |
| Select |

| Bring to Front Shift Ctrl+] |
| Bring Forward   Ctrl+] |
| Send Backward   Ctrl+[|
| Send to Back Shift Ctrl+] |
| Send to Current Layer |

- Draw a square, a circle and a star with the **Shape Tools**

When objects are drawn in Adobe Illustrator they are arranged in layers according to the order in which they have been drawn. That is: in the first illustration we can see that the square was drawn before the star and circle

- In order to change the layer order, select the object that needs to be changed
- Right click the mouse. A sub-menu will appear
- Select **Arrange**

- **Bring to Front**
  Hot Key **Ctrl Shift]** Apple OS **Cmd Shift]**
- Brings object all the way to the top

- **Bring Forward**
  Hot Key **Ctrl]** Apple OS Cmd]
- Brings object to the top one layer at a time

- **Send Backward**
  Hot Key **Ctrl [** Apple **OS Cmd [**
- Sends object to the back one layer at a time

- **Send to Back**
  Hot Key **Ctrl Shift [** Apple OS **Cmd Shift [**
- Sends object all the way to the back

Align, Distribute And Space:

Selection Tool Hot Key **V**
Ellipse Tool Hot Key **L**

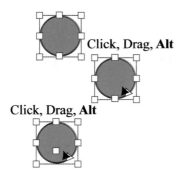

Click, Drag, **Alt**

Click, Drag, **Alt**

- Select the **Ellipse Tool** Hot Key **L**, holding down the **Shift** key, draw one circle
- With the circle still highlighted, start to drag the circle and then press the **Alt** key to copy the circle, a double arrow will appear (▶)
- Repeat this process once more to copy the circle again

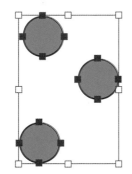

- Marquee over all three circles to select them

Align   **Distribute**

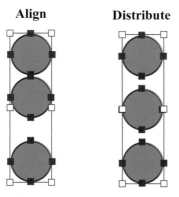

- Check if the Align option box is still open, if not click onto **Window** in the menu bar
- A drop down menu will appear
- Select **Align**
- Once the box is open select **Horizontal Align Left**
- This aligns the objects to the left
- To space the objects evenly, click onto **Vertical Distribute Centre** - this will distribute the objects evenly using the top and bottom objects as the anchors

Or:

- Click onto **Vertical Distribute Space** to even the space between objects

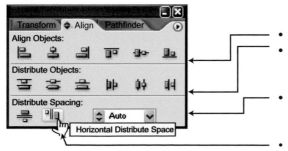

- **Align Objects** - aligns objects in a straight line
- **Distribute Objects** - distributes objects from the centre using the centre of the object as the pivotal point
- **Distribute Spacing** - distributes the space between objects, using the edge of the object as the guide

- When the cursor is resting on the icon a description of the icon will appear - all icons are suggestive of their respective functions

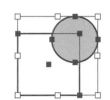

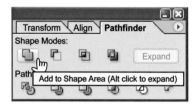

Add To Shape and Divide Objects:

Rectangle Tool Hot Key **M**
Ellipse Tool Hot Key **L**
Selection Tool Hot Key **V**
Direct Selection Tool Hot Key **A**

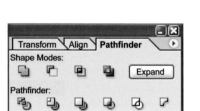

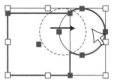

- Select white for the fill box and black for the stroke box ( )
- Select the **Rectangle Tool** Hot Key **M** and draw a square
- Select grey for the fill box and black for the stroke box ( )
- Select the **Ellipse Tool** Hot Key **L** and draw a circle
- Marquee over both the square and circle with the **Selection Tool** Hot Key **V** to select them
- The **Pathfinder** palette will have opened at the same time as the Align palette
- Once the box is open select **Add To Shape Area** This merges two or more shapes into one At this stage the individual shapes can still be moved using the **Direct Selection Tool** Hot Key **A**

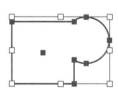

write does this in 1 step

- **Expand** the merged shapes to create one single shape

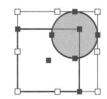

- Select white for the fill box and black for the stroke box ( )
- Select the **Rectangle Tool** Hot Key **M** and draw a square
- Select grey for the fill box and black for the stroke box ( )
- Select the **Ellipse Tool** Hot Key **L** and draw a circle
- Marquee over both the square and circle with the **Selection Tool** Hot Key **V** to select them
- Click onto the **Divide** icon in the **Pathfinder** palette This will divide the shapes The shapes are grouped after this process
- **Ungroup** the divided shapes

Ungroup the objects:

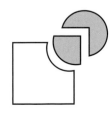

- Select the grouped object
- Right click the mouse
- A sub-menu will appear
- Select **Ungroup**
-

Or

- Press Hot key **Shift Ctrl G** Apple OS **Shift Cmd G**

Add To Shape And Divide Objects Continued:

Rectangle Tool Hot Key **M**
Ellipse Tool Hot Key **L**
Selection Tool Hot Key **V**
Direct Selection Tool Hot Key **A**
Scissor Tool Hot Key **C**
Zoom Tool Hot Key **Z**

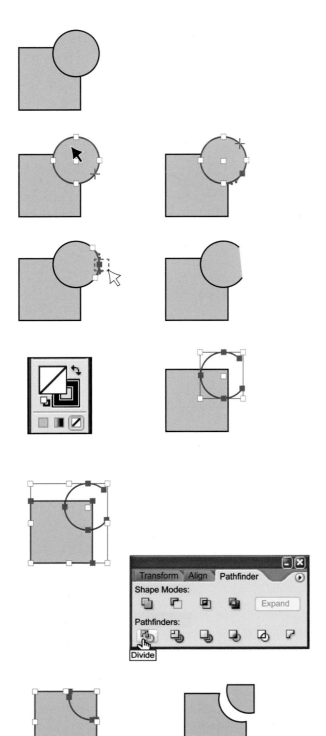

- Select grey for the fill box and black in the stroke box ( )
- Select the **Rectangle Tool** Hot Key **M** and draw a square
- Select the **Ellipse Tool** Hot Key **L** and draw a circle
- Select the circle with the **Selection Tool** Hot Key **V**
- Click onto the **Scissor Tool** Hot Key **C**
- Zoom in to the objects **Zoom Tool** Hot Key **Z** Hot Key **Ctrl +** Apple OS **Cmd +** to zoom in
- Place the centre of the cursor over the highlighted line and click outside the intersection of the circle and square. This will cut the shape
- Move the cursor along the line and repeat this again
- Click onto the **Direct Selection Tool** Hot Key **A,** marquee through the middle of the two cut points and press the **Delete** key, to delete the highlighted segment
- Select the segmented circle with the **Selection Tool** Hot Key **V**, bring the fill box to the front Hot Key **X**, remove the fill Hot Key **/** ( )
- Marquee over both the square and partial line of the circle with the **Selection Tool** Hot Key **V**

- Click onto the **Divide** icon in the **Pathfinders** option box
- This will divide the square with the segment of the circle
  The two segments are grouped after this process
- **Ungroup** the divided object

  To **Ungroup** the objects:

- Select the grouped object
- Right click the mouse
  A sub-menu will appear
- Select **Ungroup** or simply press Hot key **Shift Ctrl G** Apple OS **Shift Cmd G** and the objects will be ungrouped

Note the difference between dividing two shapes and dividing a shape with a line

17

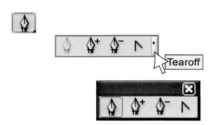

Pen Tool Options:

Pen Tool Hot Key **P**
Add Anchor Point Tool Hot Key **+**
Delete Anchor Point Tool Hot Key **-**
Convert Anchor Point Tool Hot Key **Shift C**

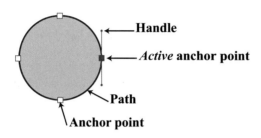

- Select the **Pen Tool** Hot Key **P**
- Click onto the black arrow at the corner to access the **Tear off** options

- An image is created with **Strokes** and **Fills**
- **Anchor Points** are joined to create **Paths** (lines) and **Paths** are joined to create objects
- A curve is determined by the length and direction of the **Handles** on one or both sides of an **Anchor Point**

← **Handle**

← *Active* **anchor point**

Path

Anchor point

Add Anchor Point Tool Hot Key **+**

- This tool adds an anchor point to a path, the anchor point can then be manipulated as needed

Delete Anchor Point Tool Hot Key **-**

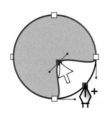

- This tool deletes anchor points from an object

Convert Anchor Point Tool Hot Key **Shift C**

- This tool manipulates anchor points and handles by clicking onto an anchor point, the handles will be removed and the anchor point becomes a point

- By activating the anchor point with the **Direct Selection Tool** Hot Key **A**, the handles become visible and the **Convert Anchor Point Tool** can be used to manipulate the **Handles**

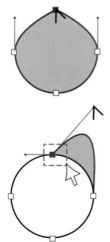

1

 2

 3

 4

Pen Tool Details:

- The **Pen Tool** pointer has four indicators that communicate different messages and they are:

  1. The cross next to the pointer appears when the **Pen Tool** is first selected

  2. This symbol indicates that the **Pen Tool** has not been deselected when the pointer is rested on the last anchor point. It is also used to create a point when clicked onto the anchor point again

  3. The forward slash next to the pointer appears if you have deselected the **Pen Tool** and then re-selected it again and want to connect to an open end point

  4. The circle denotes that two anchor points are either joined or a shape is closed

Drawing A Simple Straight Line Shape:

Pen Tool Hot Key **P**
Selection Tool Hot Key **V**

- Select black for the **Stroke** and **None** in the **Fill** Hot Key / ( )

- Click onto the **Pen Tool** Hot Key **P**
- Click the pointer onto the work area, release and move the pointer to the right, holding **Shift** at the same time and click again

  *Holding down **Shift** before the next anchor point is created will create a straight vertical or horizontal line or 45° angle line*

- Release, move the pointer down (vertically) holding **Shift** at the same time and click again

- Release and deselect the **Pen Tool** by clicking onto the **Selection Tool** Hot Key **V**

- Rest the pointer onto the last anchor point until the forward slash appears and click onto the anchor point, move the pointer up to join the first anchor point and close the shape

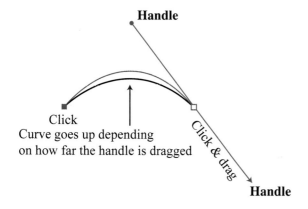

Pen Tool Hot Key **P**
Selection Tool Hot Key **V**
Direct Selection Tool Hot Key **A**

*Drawing curves with the **Pen Tool** requires a click and drag technique. When dragging the pointer after clicking, **handles** will appear on either side of the **anchor point**. The shape of a curve depends on the length and position of the **handles***

- Make sure there is still nothing in the **Fill** box Hot Key / and black in the **Stroke** (⬚)
- Click onto the **Pen Tool** Hot Key **P**

Demonstration 1: Drawing Curves With A Point Between The Curves

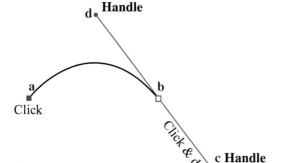

- Click onto the work area **a** and release
- Move the cursor and click **b**, do not release
- Hold down left mouse button and drag as indicated in the illustration, a **Handle** will appear **c**. This will determine the shape of the curve
- The shape of the curve will be determined by the opposite **Handle d** to the **Handle** being dragged

- To determine that the cursor is exactly on the anchor point, the **Convert Anchor Point Tool** symbol (⬚) will appear when you rest the cursor in the correct position, only once the symbol appears - click again onto **b**
- Move the cursor again and click **e**, do not release
- Hold down left mouse button and drag - a **Handle** will appear **f**. This will determine the shape of the curve
- The shape of the curve will be determined by the opposite handle to the handle being dragged **g**
- By converting the anchor point at **b**, a point has been created
- Deselect the **Pen Tool** by clicking onto the **Selection Tool** Hot Key **V**

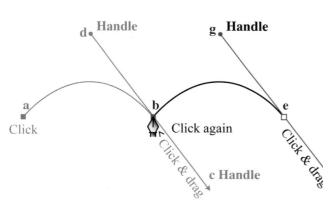

!REMEMBER!
Save the file Hot Key **Ctrl S** Apple OS **Cmd S**

Demonstration 2: Drawing A Smooth Curve

- Click onto the work area **a** and release
- Move the cursor again and click **b**, do not release
- Hold down left mouse button and drag the handle down towards **c**
- The shape of the curve will be determined by the opposite **Handle d**
- The next curve is determined by the handle being dragged with the mouse **c**

- Move the cursor again and click **e**, do not release
- Hold down left mouse button and drag the handle up towards **f**
- The shape of the curve will be determined by the opposite **Handle g**
- The next curve is determined by the handle being dragged with the mouse **f**

Demonstration 3: Re-Shaping Curved Lines

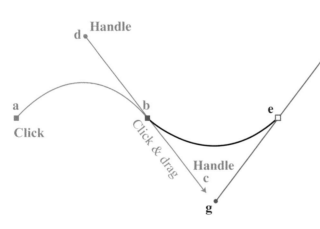

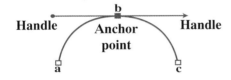

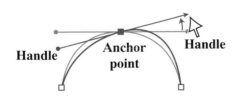

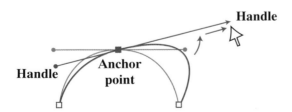

- Click onto the work area **a** and release
- Click again **b** and drag the mouse to **c**
- Click again **d**
- Select the **Direct Selection Tool** Hot Key **A**
- Marquee over the **Anchor Point** to activate the **Handles** either side of the **Anchor Point**

- Place the **Direct Selection Tool** at the end of the **Handle** and move the **Handle** up or down
  *This will move the **Handles** in a see-saw manner affecting both sides of the curve*

- The curve can also be re-shaped by lengthening or shortening the Handle
- Place the **Direct Selection Tool** at the end of the Handle and draw the Handle out or in to adjust the curve
- Do *not* deselect the **Anchor Point**

Convert Anchor Point Tool Hot Key **Shift C**
Selection Tool Hot Key **V**

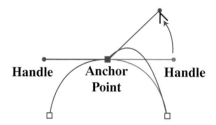

Handle   Anchor   Handle
          Point

- Click onto the **Convert Anchor Point Tool**
  Hot Key **Shift C**

- Click onto the end of the handle and move the
  Handle

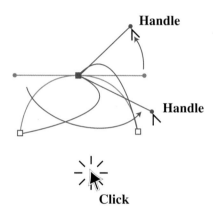

Handle

Handle

Click

- The **Handles** either side of the **Anchor Point** can
  now be manipulated separately, effectively forming
  a point at the **Anchor Point**

- To finish, select the **Selection Tool** Hot Key **V** and
  click onto the work area

  You are now ready to draw a simple shape!

Step 1: Drag A Guide Onto The Working Surface

Selection Tool Hot Key **V**

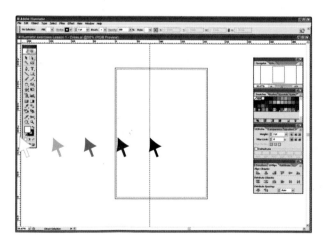

- Click into the vertical ruler area
- Holding the right mouse button down, drag to the
  right and a vertical guide line will appear
- The default settings for the guide line will mean
  that it is automatically locked
- To view the status of the guide lines click onto
  View in the menu bar
  ⟶ **Guides**
- A sub-menu with options will appear - the **Lock
  Guides** option will be ticked

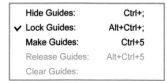

Hide Guides:	Ctrl+;
✓ Lock Guides:	Alt+Ctrl+;
Make Guides:	Ctrl+5
Release Guides:	Alt+Ctrl+5
Clear Guides:	

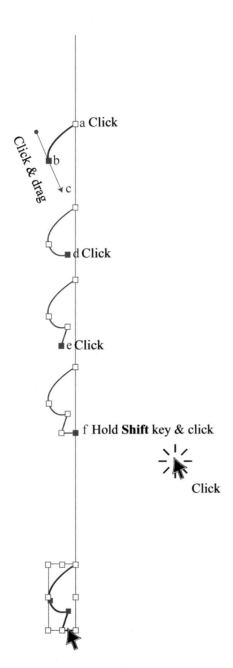

a Click

Click & drag

b

c

d Click

e Click

f Hold **Shift** key & click

Click

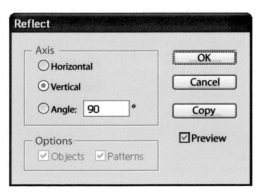

Reflect

Axis
- ○ Horizontal
- ◉ Vertical
- ○ Angle: 90 °

Options
- ☑ Objects ☑ Patterns

- OK
- Cancel
- Copy

☑ Preview

Step 2: Create Half The Shape

Pen Tool Hot Key **P**
Selection Tool Hot Key **V**

- Click onto the **Pen Tool** Hot Key **P**
- Make sure there is still nothing in the **Fill** box Hot Key / and black in the **Stroke** ( )
- Click onto the locked **Guide Line a**, release
- Move the cursor and click **b**, do *not* release
- Hold down left mouse button and drag - a **Handle** will appear **c**, release
  *Remember, when dragging the **Handle,** the line you can see is being shaped by the opposite handle to the handle being dragged - this **Handle (c)** determines the shape of the line still to be created*
- Move the cursor and click **d**, release

- Move the cursor and click **e**, release

- Hold down **Shift** and click onto the **Guide Line f**, release
  This creates a straight horizontal line
- Half the shape is complete
- Select the **Selection Tool** Hot Key **V** and click onto the work area
  *This will deactivate the **Pen Tool***

Step 3: Reflect And Copy The Shape

Selection Tool Hot Key **V**

- Select the shape with the **Selection Tool** Hot Key **V**

- Right click the mouse - a pop-up menu will appear
- Click onto **Transform** and then **Reflect**

- A dialogue box will appear

- For the purpose of this exercise select **Vertical** and **90°** in **Axis** box
  Vertical will copy from left to right as opposed to horizontal which copies from top to bottom

- Click onto the **Preview** box ( ) to preview the action
- **Copy**
- Do *not* deselect the shape

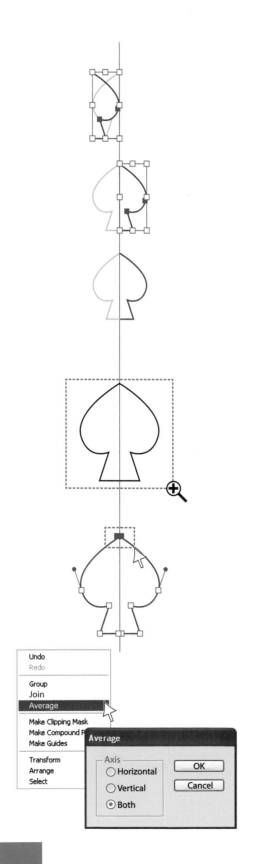

Step 4: Move The Shape

Selection Tool Hot Key **V**

- Hold down the right mouse button and start to drag the shape to the right
- Only after having selected and starting to move the shape, press the **Shift** key to drag the shape in a straight line - 180°

- Using the arrow direction keys on the keyboard, nudge the shape into place

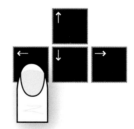

- Deselect

Step 5: Average The Two Halves

Direct Selection Tool Hot Key **A**
Zoom Tool Hot Key **Z**

- Select the **Zoom Tool** Hot Key **Z** and marquee over the shape to magnify it
- Click onto the **Direct Selection Tool** Hot Key **A**
- Marquee over the two open end points at the top of the shape

- Right click the mouse

- A pop-up menu will appear

- Select Average

- Select **Both** (⊙), to place the two points on top of each other

- Do *not* deselect

Step 6: Join The Two Halves

Direct Selection Tool Hot Key **A**
Selection Tool Hot Key **V**

- The Anchor Points are still selected

- Right click the mouse

- A pop-up menu will appear

- Select **Join**
- Select **Corner** (◉), to join the two points
- **OK**
- Deselect

- Repeat this procedure for the bottom open end points
- Once that is done the shape is a closed shape

- Click onto the stroke (line), with the **Selection Tool** Hot Key **V** to select the shape

- Select a fill colour from the **Swatches** palette ()

- Remove the **Guide Line** by clicking onto **View** in the menu bar
  ⟶ **Guides**
- A sub-menu with options will appear

- Select **Clear Guides**

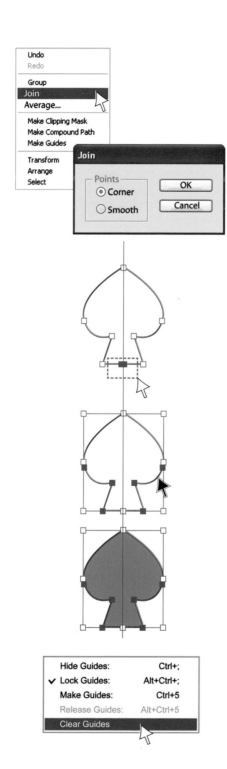

!REMEMBER!
Save the file Hot Key **Ctrl S** Apple OS **Cmd S**

TYPE TOOL

Type Tool:

Type Tool Hot Key **T**
Type Palette Hot Key **Ctrl T** Apple OS **Cmd T**

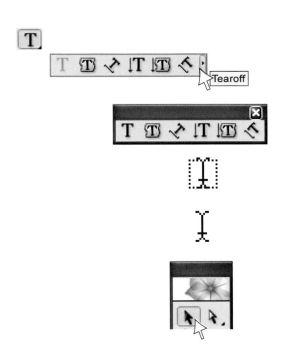

- Open the **Type Tool** palette, by clicking onto the arrow at the corner of the type tool box and drag the cursor along the **Type Tools,** to the end of the icons
- A **Tear off** option will appear when the cursor reaches the end of the icons

- A type symbol will come up, denoting that the type tool has been selected but not activated

- By clicking onto the work area, the type tool is activated and a flashing line will appear

- The only way to deselect the type tool is to click onto the **Selection Tool** in the tool box
- Do not use the Hot Key, as this is read as a letter when the **Type Tool** is activated

- There are 6 different options in the type tool

Type Tool Hot Key **T:**

Types in a straight, horizontal line

- This is the basic type tool, select this option and click onto the work area and start typing

Area Type Tool:

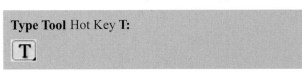

- This tool adds text within a closed shape. Select this option and click onto the edge of the shape, the outline of the area will go transparent and start to type or paste imported text

Type On A Path Tool:

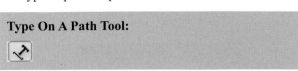

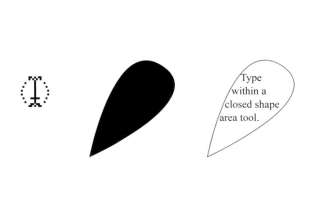

- This tool types along a designated line (path). Select this option and click onto the path, the line will go transparent and type along the path

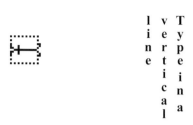

Vertical Type Tool:

- This type tool types vertically. Select this option and click onto the work area and start typing

Vertical Area Type Tool:

- This tool does the same as the area type tool, but types vertically
  Note: this type method will type from right to left

Vertical Type On A Path Tool:

- This tool does the same as the path type tool, but types vertically

Moving Type On A Path:

Selection Tool Hot Key **V**
Direct Selection Tool Hot Key **A**

- Select the type with the **Selection Tool** Hot Key **V**
- Click onto the **Direct Selection Tool** Hot Key **A** and carefully place the cursor onto the fine line at the start of the type and move
  This will move the type along the path

- By carefully placing the cursor onto the fine line in the middle of the type, it will then flip the type onto the other side of the path

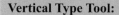

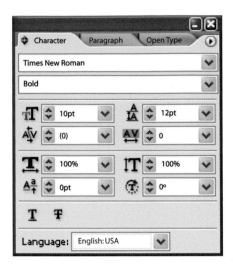

To Open The Type Tool Palette:
Type Palette Hot Key **Ctrl T** Apple OS **Cmd T**

- Clicking onto Hot Key **Ctrl T** Apple OS **Cmd T** will open the **Type Tool** palette
- The **Type Tool** palette has sub-palettes
- **Character** - in this palette the font can be selected and size and spacing is determined

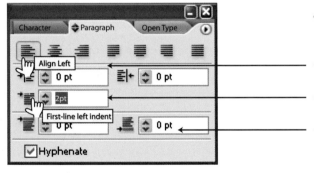

- **Paragraph** - in this palette paragraph alignment and style can be determined

- Resting the cursor over the option will reveal the name of the option
- Clicking into the option measurements allows the user to change the measurement
- Clicking onto the arrows makes the measurements higher (▲) or lower (▼)

*Note: The program default is set linking **Character**;* ***Paragraph** and **Open Type** to open at the same time*

Chapter one is complete.
You now have enough understanding of the different tools to create a simple garment.

CHAPTER 2

FIRST GARMENT

Chapter 2 is step-by-step practical instructions of how to apply the information from Chapter One to drawing a simple garment. In this chapter we also introduce simple pattern fills, brush strokes and a simple technical drawing.

Drawing A Simple Garment

*   From *Adobe Illustrator* Click onto **File** in the
    menu bar
    New Hot Key **Ctrl N**   Apple OS **Cmd N**
    An option box will appear - do not name file
    Artboard Setup
    Select Size: A4
    Orientation: Portrait (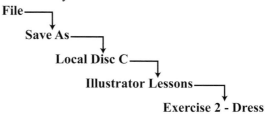**)**
    RGB Color (◉)
    OK
*   Immediately save the file
    File
            Save As
                    Local Disc C
                            Illustrator Lessons
                                    Exercise 2 - Dress

    *This will save the file into the directory originally
    set up on page 5*

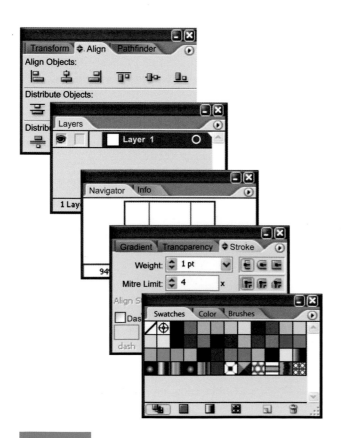

*   Click onto **View** in the menu bar
*   Click onto **Show Rulers**
    Hot Key **Ctrl R** Apple OS **Cmd R**

*   Show Palettes: (Refer to pages 4 and 5)

*   Click onto **View** in the menu bar and click onto:
    ➤windows
    Align - Pathfinder, Transform
    Layers
    Navigator - Info
    Stroke - Gradient, Transparency
    Swatches - Color, Brushes
    Tools - These will have come up as a default when
    you opened the new file

    Clicking onto any of the linked palettes -
    ***Align, Navigator, Stroke and Swatches** - will
    automatically bring up the other linked palettes*

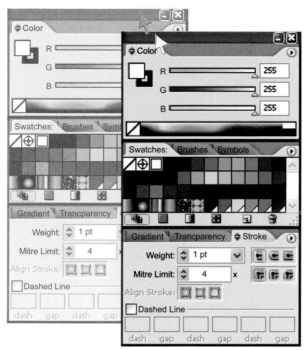

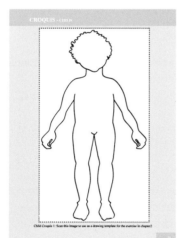

Creating Space In The Work Area

- Place the cursor in the blue bar to move the palette
- Minimise palettes for more space

- Click onto the red cross ( ) in the right hand corner to close the palette

- To toggle between the minimise and maximise:
  Click onto the blue line ( ) in the right hand corner to minimise the palette
  Click onto the blue square ( ) in the right hand corner to maximise the palette

- Hide all palettes and leave the **Tool Box** visible by pressing Hot Key **Shift Tab**,
- Press Hot Key **Shift Tab** again to show all palettes

Step 3: Scan In Child Croquis 1

- Scan in the image on Page 71 and save as a JPEG or a TIFF file
  onto your **C Drive**

  Adobe Illustrator Exercises

  Child Croquis 1 Scan

- Please note all scanners are different and there are two points to consider:
  1) Scan the image at 150 DPI (Dots Per Inch)
  2) Scan the image in black and white - this makes it a smaller file
- For all other instructions follow the scanner instructions
  If drawing your own figure, it is essential there are no gaps in the lines

Step 4: Place Scanned Croquis

- Click onto **File** in the menu bar
- Select **Place**
- The same directory where the **Exercise 2 - Dress** file was saved will open
- Select the **Child Croquis 1 Scan file**
  This will place the scanned image into the open file

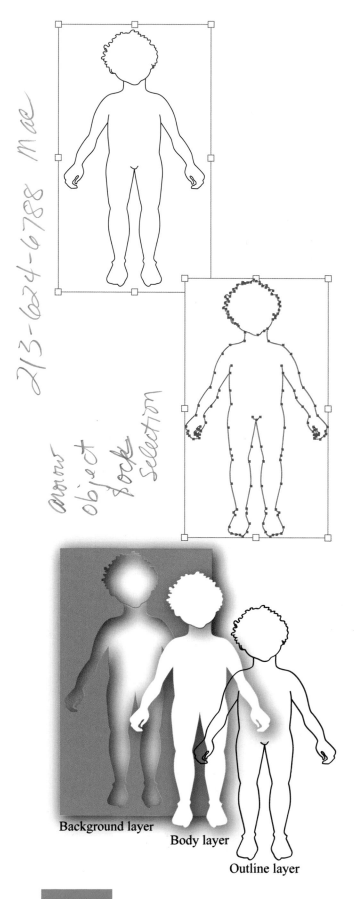

Background layer

Body layer

Outline layer

Step 5: Trace Scanned Image

- Select the scanned image which is a *Bitmap Image*
- Click onto the arrow next to **Live Trace** in the menu bar

- A drop-down menu will appear

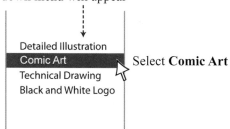

Select **Comic Art**

- The image will be traced and now needs to be expanded to create a *Vector Image*

Step 6: Expand The Traced Image

- Once the image is traced an option to **Expand** the image will appear in the tool bar

- Click onto this option and the image will become a vector image
- Deselect the image

Detail Of The Traced Image:

- Once the image is traced and expanded it can be ungrouped into layers of shapes
- **Background Layer**: this is the area around the scanned image
- **Body Layer**: this is the fill inside the outline
- **Outline Layer**: this is the line around the body
  - *note: this is not* **stroke**, *but a* **fill**.

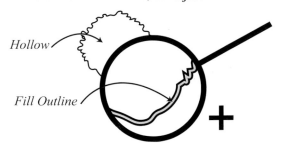

Hollow

Fill Outline

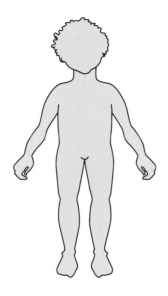

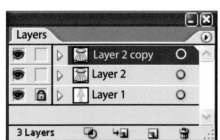

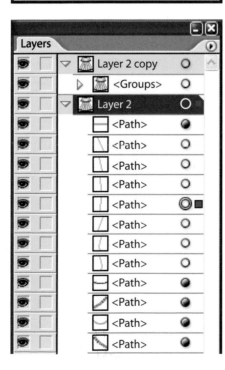

Step 7: Change The Colour Of The Figure

Selection Tool Hot Key **V**

- Select the background layer and **Delete** the layer with the **Selection Tool** Hot Key **V**
- Click onto the body, hold the **Shift** key down and click onto the head with the **Selection Tool**
- Go to the **Swatches** palette and select a flesh colour

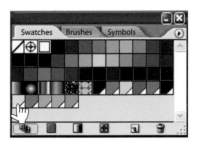

Layers:

- The **Layers Palette** gives you the option to store different parts of a story board on different layers
- To open **Layers** click onto **Window** in the tool bar
- A drop down menu will appear and select **Layers** to show palette
- **Layer 1** has the croquis (template)
- **Layer 2** has colour 1 of the dress
- **Layer 2 copy** has colour 2 of the dress
- The eye (👁) denotes the layer is visible
- To *hide* the layer, click onto the eye and the layer will become invisible (☐)
- The padlock (🔒) denotes the layer is locked
- To *unlock* the layer, click onto the padlock and the layer will be unlocked and can be worked on (☐)
- To create a new layer click onto the **New Layer** icon (▣)
- To delete a layer, select the layer and then click onto the waste basket (🗑) and the highlighted layer will be deleted
- Each layer has **Sub-layers**
- Click onto the arrow (▷) to reveal the sub-layers
- If the objects are grouped, there will be as many sub-layers as there are grouped objects
- All objects will have as many sub-layers as there are operations in the object
- Any part of the object can be selected by double clicking onto the circle (◎ ■) in the layer, click again onto the circle to deselect (○)

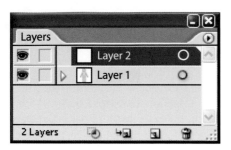

- Create a new layer in the **Layers** palette, by clicking onto the **Create New Layer** icon (⬛)
- This is the layer the garment will be created in
- The layer that is being used will be highlighted with a blue bar

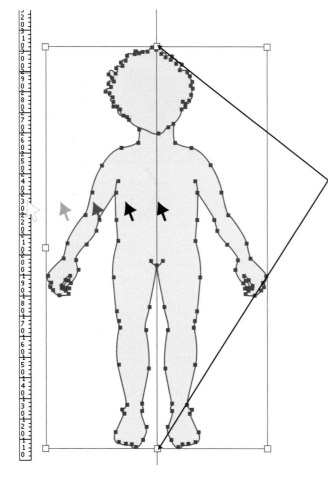

- Select **Layer 1** again by clicking onto the **Layer 1** bar and select the whole figure
- Click onto **Layer 2** again
- Using the centre of the bounding box as a guide, place the cursor into the vertical ruler and drag a guide line to the centre of the figure

- Select **Layer 1** again by clicking onto the **Layer 1** bar
- **Lock** the layer (🔒)
  The layer cannot be edited while this icon is visible

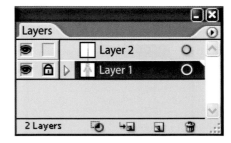

- Select **Layer 2** again to begin drawing the garment

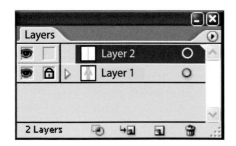

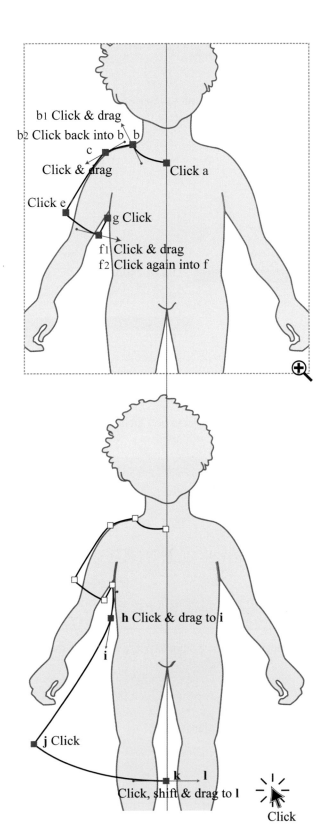

Pen Tool Hot Key **P**

- Select the **Pen Tool** Hot Key **P**
- Make sure there is nothing in the **Fill** box Hot Key / and black in the **Stroke** ()
- Click onto the **Guide Line a**, release
- Move the cursor, click and drag **b1**, release
- Click again onto the same anchor point **b2**, - this will create a point
- Move the cursor, click and drag **c**, release
- Move the cursor and click **e**, release
- Move the cursor, click and drag **f1**, release
- Click again onto the same anchor point **f2** - this will create a point
- Move the cursor and click **g**, release

Step 11: Complete One Half Of The Dress

Pen Tool Hot Key **P**
Selection Tool Hot Key **V**
Hand Tool Hot Key **H**

- Click **h** and drag in the direction of the next anchor point **i**, release
- Move the cursor and click **j**, release
- Move the cursor and click onto the guide line **k**, do not release, hold down left mouse button and **Shift** key, at the same time drag to the right, a handle will appear **l**, release
- Deselect the **Pen Tool** by clicking onto the **Selection Tool** Hot Key **V**
- Click away from the garment shape to deselect

- To move around the work area, click onto the **Hand Tool** Hot Key **H**

Or:

- Just hold down the Space Bar, a hand () will appear. Hold the left mouse button down and move around the work area

By using the Hot Key for the above operation, this allows you to remain in the tool being used once the Hot Key is released

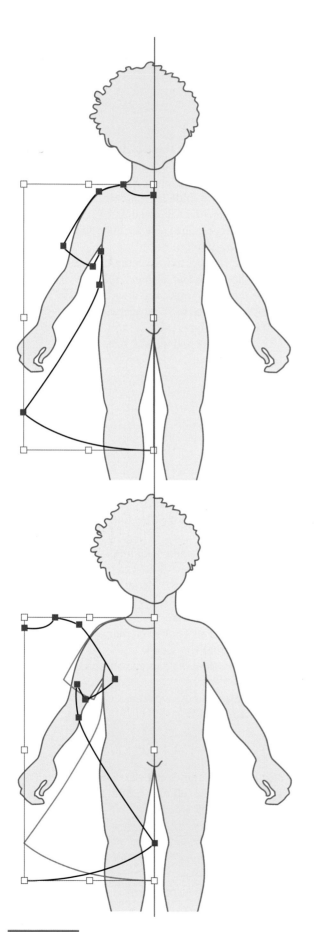

- Select the dress with the **Selection Tool** Hot Key **V**
- Right click the mouse - a pop-up menu will appear

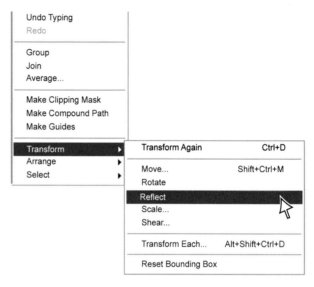

- Click onto **Transform** and then **Reflect**
- A dialogue box will appear

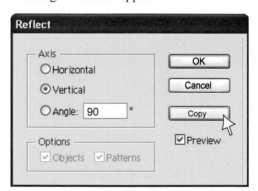

- For the purpose of this exercise select **Vertical** (◉) in the Axis box
- **90**° will show up next to **Angle**
- To preview the operation, tick (☑) the **Preview** box
- **Copy**
- Do *not* deselect the shape

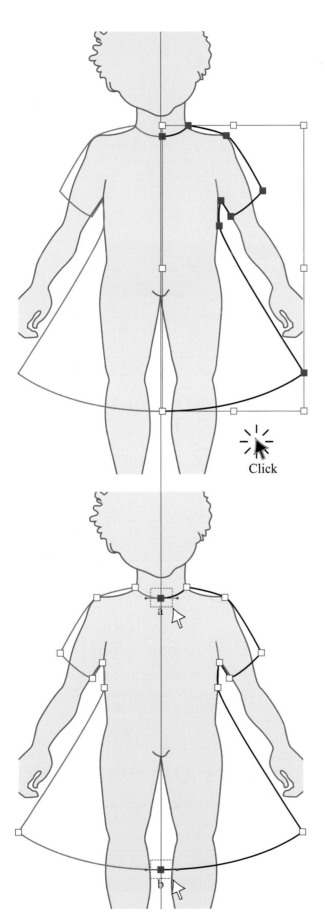

Click

Selection Tool Hot Key **V**

- Hold down the left mouse button and start to drag the shape to the right
- Only after having selected and starting to move the shape, press the **Shift** key to drag the shape in a straight line - 180°
- Use the arrow direction keys on the keyboard to nudge the shape into place
- Deselect the dress by clicking away from the shape
  *At this point it would be useful to check for and delete **Stray Anchor Points** - these are individual anchor points that are not connected to other anchor points.*

- *Deselect all objects.*

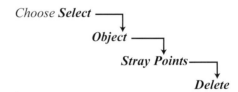

*Choose **Select***
Object
Stray Points
Delete

Direct Selection Tool Hot Key **A**

- Marquee over the points at the centre neck **a** with the **Direct Selection Tool** Hot Key **A**
- Ensure that only the two points to be joined are highlighted
- Right mouse click, a pop-up menu will appear, click onto **Average**
- A dialogue box will appear
- Select **Both** (⊙)
- **OK**
- This will place the two points on top of each other
- Do not deselect
- Right click the mouse again, a pop-up menu will appear
- Click onto **Join**
- A dialogue box will appear
- Select **Corner** (⊙)
- **OK**
- This will join the two points
- Repeat the same process for **b**

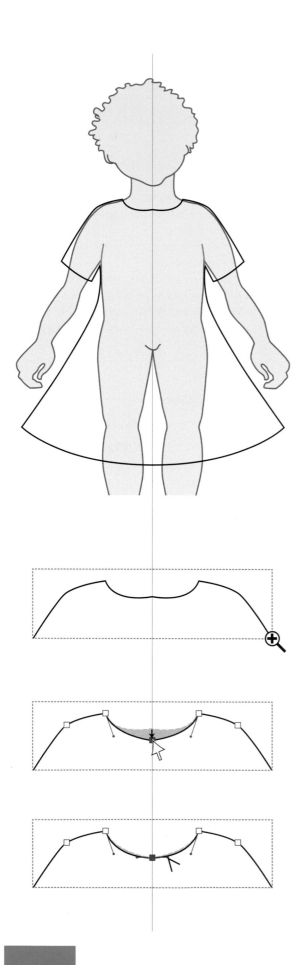

Selection Tool Hot Key **V**

- Now that the basic shape is complete the croquis layer does not need to be visible
- Leave Layer 1 locked and click onto the eye (👁)
- This will hide the layer (☐)
  Hidden layers do not print

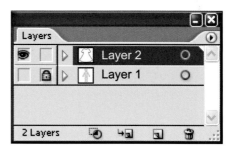

- Remember to click onto Layer 2 to continue

Step 16: Smooth The Neck Join

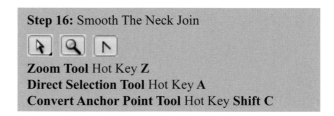

Zoom Tool Hot Key **Z**
Direct Selection Tool Hot Key **A**
Convert Anchor Point Tool Hot Key **Shift C**

- Zoom up to the centre join of the neckline

- Select the **Direct Selection Tool** Hot Key **A**
- Click onto the centre anchor point, hold the **Shift** key down and drag the cursor down

- Select the **Convert Anchor Point Tool** Hot Key **Shift C**
- Click onto the centre anchor point, hold the **Shift** key down and drag the cursor to the left
- **Handles** will appear either side of the anchor point
- Holding the **Shift** key will ensure that the handles are dragged evenly in straight line
- This will smooth the join at the centre front neck point

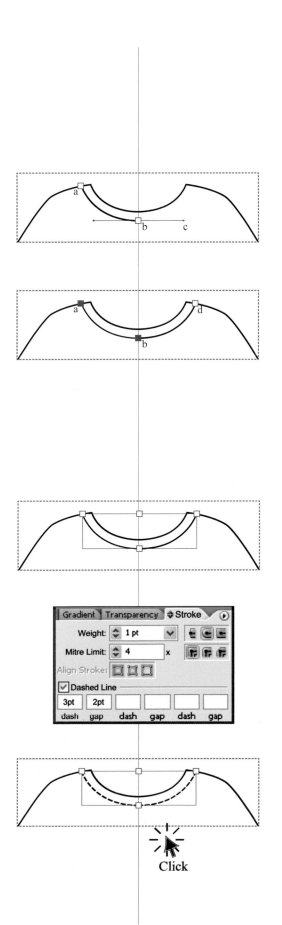

Step 17: Adding Top Stitching

Pen Tool Hot Key **P**

- Select the **Pen Tool** Hot Key **P**
- Click onto the shoulder **a**
- Click onto the centre guide line **b**
- Hold down both the left mouse button and **Shift** key, at the same time drag to the right **c** - this will create a symmetrical curve
- Release the **Shift** key

- Click onto the right shoulder **d**

Step 18: Creating A Dashed Line

Selection Tool Hot Key **V**

- Click onto the **Selection Tool** Hot Key **V**
- Select the line

- To create a dashed line, go to the **Stroke** palette
- Tick (☑) the **Dashed Line** box
- Fill numeric values in the dash and gap boxes
- For example **3pt dash** and **2pt gap**
- Select the round cap (◉)
- Check that the **Stroke Weight** is **1pt**

- Click away to deselect the line
- To continue remove the tick (▣) from the dashed line box

Click

!REMEMBER!
Zoom For Details

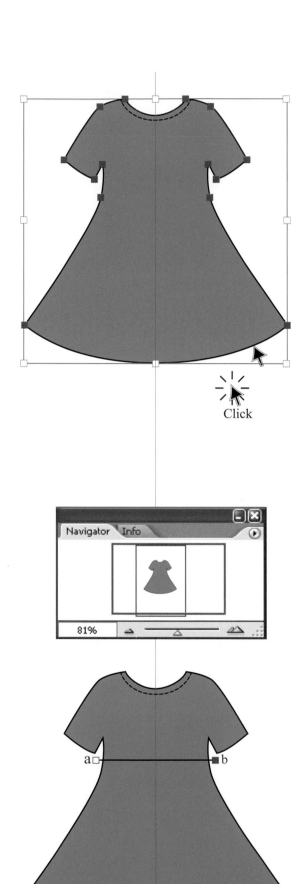

Click

Step 19: Add Colour Fill

Selection Tool Hot Key **V**

- Click onto the **Selection Tool** Hot Key **V**
- Click onto the dress - *be sure that the cursor is exactly on the **Stroke** line, as the dress will not be selected if you click into the centre, as there is nothing to select*
- Bring the fill box to the front Hot Key **X** (⬚)

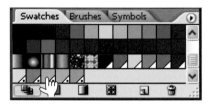

- Select a **Fill** colour from the **Swatches** palette (⬚)
- Click away to deselect

Step 20: Draw The Divide Line

Pen Tool Hot Key **P**
Navigator Palette

Reminder - Navigator allows you to *navigate* around the specified working area, by clicking on the window and moving, a hand (🖐) will appear or by using the zoom sliding bar at the bottom of the box

- Select the **Pen Tool** Hot Key **P**
- Bring the fill box to the front Hot Key **X**
- Remove the colour from the fill box Hot Key / *It is important not to have any colour in the fill box when using a line to divide, as a line with colour will be treated like a shape. This would be noticeable in a shaped line*
- Click outside the dress shape **a**
- Press the **Shift** key and click again outside the dress shape on the other side **b** - this creates a horizontal line

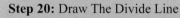

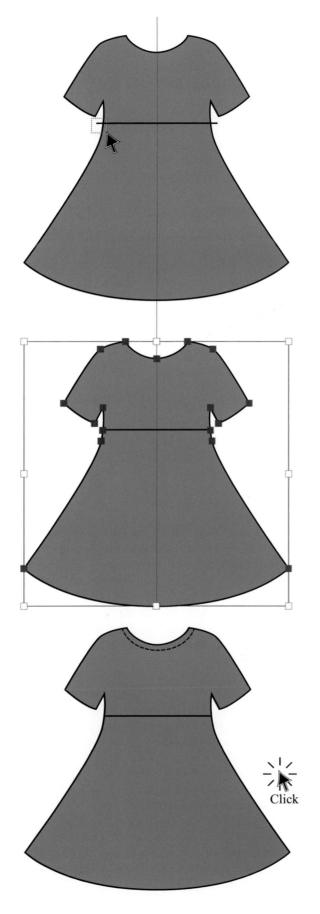

Step 21: Divide The Dress Shape

Selection Tool Hot Key **V**

- Click on the outside of the dress and marquee over the dress shape and the divide line with the **Selection Tool** Hot Key **V**
- Do not select the neck stitch line

- Note how the fill box has a question mark (?) in it now (), this confirms that the dress has a fill colour and the line has no fill

- When selected click onto the **Divide** icon ([⬚]) in the **Pathfinder** palette

Step 22: Ungroup The Dress Shape

[↖]

Selection Tool Hot Key **V**

Once the dress has been divided the dress will be on the same layer as the dividing line (refer to page 14 -Arrange Objects). The neckline top stitch is now behind the dress shape

- The dress is now two separate shapes grouped together
- Select the dress
- Right click the mouse
  A sub-menu will appear
- Select **Ungroup**

  Or

- Hot key **Shift Ctrl G Apple OS Shift Cmd G** and the dress will be ungrouped

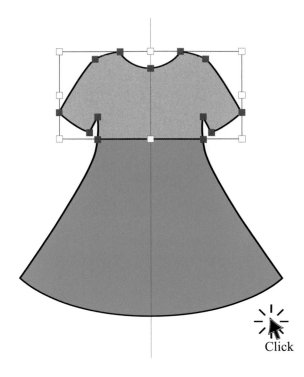

Click

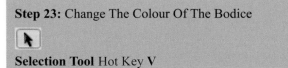

Selection Tool Hot Key **V**

- Deselect the ungrouped dress by clicking away
- Each shape can now be selected and the colour changed
- Click onto the **Selection Tool** Hot Key **V** and select the bodice shape
- Bring the fill box to the front Hot Key **X**

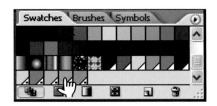

- Select a **Fill** colour from the **Swatches** palette (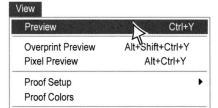)

- Click away to deselect

The Difference Between **Preview** And **Outline** View

- Up to this point we have only been working in **Preview** - this shows the artwork in colour with all attributes - colour, stroke weight, dashed line etc. It is easier to work in **Preview** as this is the true representation of the drawing, but you cannot view anything that is behind an object created later
- The neck top stitch line is behind the bodice due to dividing the dress. The divide line was drawn after the neck top stitch and once this line was used to divide the dress it brought the whole dress forward as a group

- To view the stitch line, it is necessary to go into the **Outline** view - this shows the artwork in black and white line with no attributes - colour, stroke weight, dashed line etc.
- Click onto **View** in the menu bar
- A drop down menu will appear
- Click onto **Outline** - to toggle between the **View** and **Outline** Hot Key **Ctrl Y** Apple OS **Cmd Y**

- In this view all **Stray Points** will also be visible *Stray Anchor Points - these are individual anchor points that are not connected to other anchor points.*

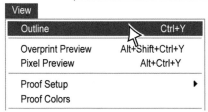

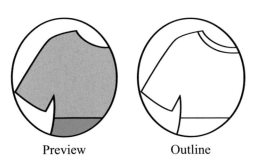

Preview   Outline

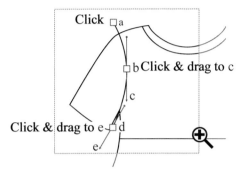

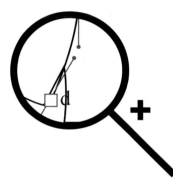

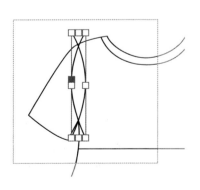

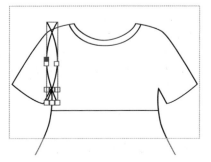

Pen Tool Hot Key **P**
Zoom Tool Hot Key **Z**
Selection Tool Hot Key **V**

- Make sure there is nothing in the **Fill** box
  Hot Key / and black in the **Stroke** ()
- Click onto **View** in the menu bar
- A drop down menu will appear
- Click onto **Outline**
- To toggle between the two:
  Hot Key **Ctrl Y** Apple OS **Cmd Y**
- Zoom up closer with the **Zoom Tool** Hot Key **Z**
- Select the **Pen Tool** Hot Key **P** and click outside
  the dress shape **a**, at the shoulder point
- Click halfway down vertically and drag the mouse
  to start creating the armhole shape **b**
- Remember to be aware of the direction and length
  of the handle **c**
- Click onto **d** outside the dress shape and drag the
  mouse to **e** - making sure that the armhole line
  intersects the dress bodice at the underarm point
- Deselect by clicking onto the
  Selection Tool Hot Key **V** and click away

Step 25: Reflect And Copy The Armhole Line

Selection Tool Hot Key **V**

- Select the armhole line with the
  Selection Tool Hot Key **V**
- Right click the mouse - a pop-up menu will appear
- Click onto **Transform** and **Reflect**
- A dialogue box will appear
- Select **Vertical** (⊙) and **90°** in the **Axis** box
- To preview the operation, tick (☑) the **Preview** box
- **Copy**
- Do not deselect the line

Step 26: Zoom Out
Hot Keys **Ctrl −** Apple OS **Cmd -** to zoom out or
Hot Keys **Ctrl +** Apple OS **Cmd +** to zoom in

- Zoom out Hot Key **Ctrl −** Apple OS **Cmd -**
  Hold **Ctrl** /Apple OS **Cmd** key down and tap the
  subtraction key until the whole bodice is visible

SELECT THE BODICE DESIGN

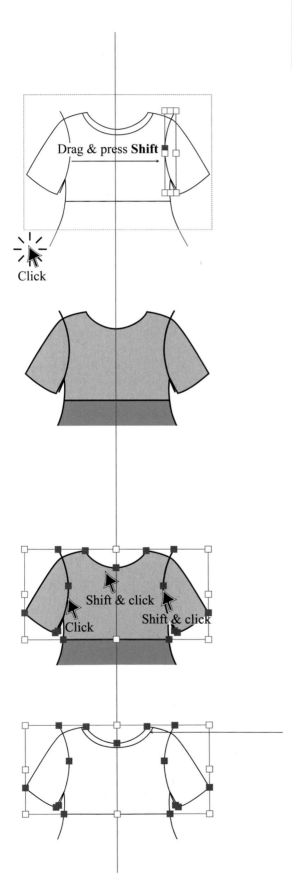

Step 27: Move The Armhole Line Across

Selection Tool Hot Key **V**

- Hold down the left mouse button and start to drag the line to the right
- Only after having selected and starting to move the line press the **Shift** key to drag the line in a straight line - **180°**
- Use the arrow direction keys on the keyboard to nudge the line into place
- Deselect the line by clicking away from the dress

Step 28: Select The Preview View
Preview Hot Key **Ctrl Y** Apple OS **Cmd Y**

- Click onto **View** in the menu bar
- A drop down menu will appear
- Click onto **Preview**
  Hot Key **Ctrl Y** Apple OS **Cmd Y**

Step 29: Select The Bodice And Armhole Design Lines

Selection Tool Hot Key **V**

- Select the left armhole line with the **Selection Tool** Hot Key **V**
- Hold down the **Shift** key and click onto the right armhole line
- Hold down the **Shift** key and select the bodice
- When you look at the **Outline View**
  Hot Key **Ctrl Y** Apple OS **Cmd Y** you will note that the neck stitching line has not been selected
  *Holding down **Shift** allows you to pick up more than one piece at a time without deselecting the previous piece.*

  *When selecting the bodice to be divided by the armhole lines, it is important not to select the neckline top stitch at the same time. Switching between **Outline** and **Preview** is a good practice to develop Hot Key Ctrl Y Apple OS Cmd Y*

!REMEMBER!
Save the file Hot Key **Ctrl S** Apple OS **Cmd S**

Selection Tool Hot Key **V**

- When the bodice and armhole lines are selected click onto the **Divide** icon () in the **Pathfinder** palette

Step 31: Arrange The Layer Order Of Objects

Selection Tool Hot Key **V**

- Click onto **Outline** view in the **View** menu Hot Key **Ctrl Y** Apple OS **Cmd Y**
- Select the neckline top stitch with the **Selection Tool** Hot Key **V**
- Right click the mouse and a pop up menu will appear
- Select **Arrange**
- Click onto **Bring To Front** Hot Key **Shift Ctrl]** Apple OS **Shift Cmd]**

Click

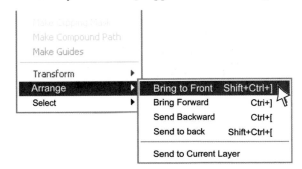

- Click away to deselect

- Click onto **Preview** again Hot Key **Ctrl Y** Apple OS **Cmd Y**

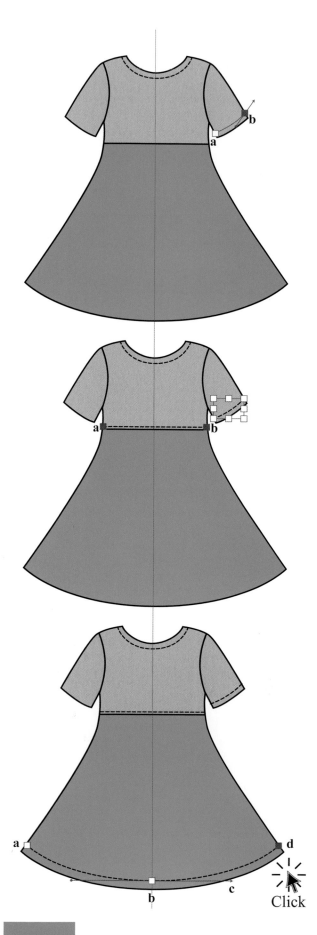

Step 32: Add Top Stitch

Pen Tool Hot Key **P**
Selection Tool Hot Key **V**

- Remove the fill colour by clicking onto the **None** box

  - Make sure the fill box is in front Hot Key **X** to bring the fill box forward
  - **None** box

- **Sleeve Hem:**
- Select the **Pen Tool** Hot Key **P**
- Click onto the underarm side of the sleeve hem about 4mm from the sleeve edge **a**
- Click onto the topside of the sleeve **b** and drag the cursor, manipulating the handle to follow the sleeve hem line

- Do not deselect the hemline
- To create a dashed line go to the **Stroke** palette
- Tick the dashed line box (☑)
- Fill in numeric values in the **dash** and **gap** boxes
- E.g.: **3pt dash** and **2pt gap**
- Select the **Round Cap** (▣)
- Check that the stroke weight is **1pt**
- Leave the **Dashed Line** ticked (☑)
- Click onto the **Selection Tool** Hot Key **V** to deselect the **Pen Tool**, *there is no need to click away*, just re-select the **Pen Tool** Hot Key **P**

- **Waist top stitch:**
- Click on the bodice side of the waist line **a**
- Press the **Shift** key and click again onto the opposite side **b**
- Click onto the **Selection Tool** Hot Key **V** to deselect the **Pen Tool**
- Re-select the **Pen Tool** Hot Key **P**

- **Skirt hem top stitch:**
- Click on the left side of the hem line **a**
- Click onto the centre guide line **b** and hold the **Shift** key down while dragging to the right **c,** until the hem shape has been copied
- Click onto the right side of the hemline **d**
- Click onto the **Selection Tool** Hot Key **V** to deselect the **Pen Tool**
- Click away from the dress to deselect
- Remove the tick from the dashed line box (☑)

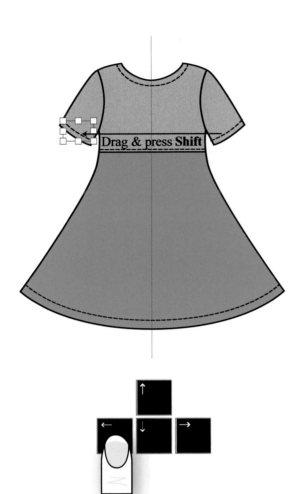

Drag & press **Shift**

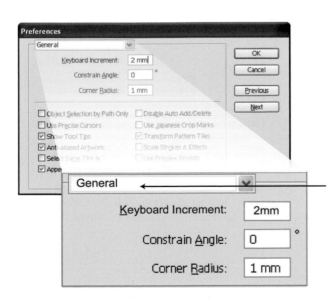

Selection Tool Hot Key **V**

- Select the sleeve hemline with the
  Selection Tool Hot Key **V**
- Right click the mouse - a pop-up menu will appear
- Click onto **Transform** and then **Reflect**
- A dialogue box will appear
- Select **Vertical** (◎) and **90°** in **Axis** box
- To preview the operation, tick (☑) the **Preview**
  box
- **Copy**
- Do not deselect the line

Selection Tool Hot Key **V**

- Hold down the left mouse button and start to drag
  the stitch line to the left
- Only *after* having selected and starting to move the
  stitch line, press the **Shift** key to drag the shape in
  a straight line - 180°
- Use the arrow direction keys on the keyboard to
  nudge the line into place

- Deselect the line by clicking away from the dress

  Remember: To **Set Keyboard Increment:**

- Click onto **Edit** in the menu bar
- Select **Preferences**
  Hot Key **Ctrl K** Apple OS **Cmd K**

- Select **General**
- Go to **Keyboard Increment**
- Type measurement into the white box - **2mm**
- **OK**
- This will move the selected object by 2mm

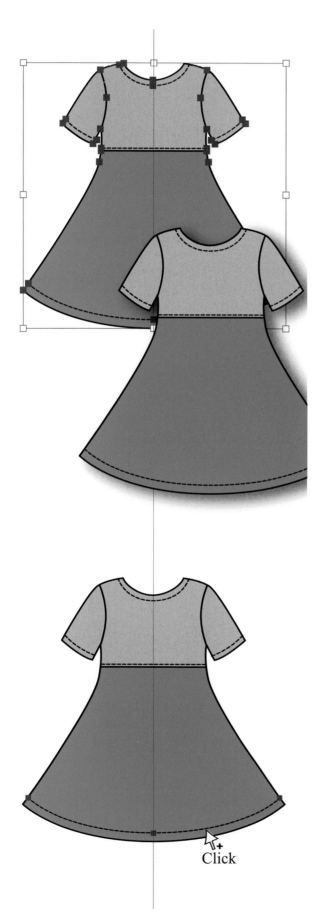

Selection Tool Hot Key **V**

- Marquee over the whole dress with the **Selection Tool** Hot Key **V**
- Right click the mouse and a pop-up menu will appear

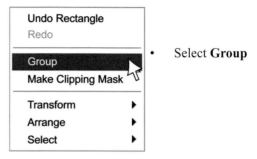

- Select **Group**

- Click away from the dress to deselect

- The simple dress shape is now complete

- You are now ready to manipulate this dress

- Make a copy of the dress Hot Key **Ctrl C**; **Ctrl V** Apple OS **Cmd C**; **Cmd V**

Step 36: To Delete The Hem Stitch Line
Group Selection Tool - no Hot Key

- Select the **Group Selection Tool**

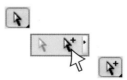

- The **Group Selection Tool** is located in behind the **Direct Selection Tool**
- Click onto the arrow in the corner and drag the cursor along to reveal the **Group Selection Tool**
- Click onto the skirt hem stitch line (as the dress is grouped, using the **Group Selection Tool** will select the hem stitch line only) and **Delete**

Click

Anchor Point Options:

Pen Tool Hot Key **P**
Add Anchor Point Tool Hot Key **+**
Delete Anchor Point Tool Hot Key **-**

- Select the **Pen Tool** Hot Key **P**
- Click onto the black arrow at the corner to access the **Tear off** options

Step 37: Add Anchor Points

Add Anchor Point Tool Hot Key **+**

- Select the **Add Anchor Point Tool** Hot Key **+**
  The Hot Key + option only works from the second row of the keyboard
- Click onto the hem stroke line to add an anchor point **a**
- It is very important to place the end of the **Add Anchor Point Tool** exactly onto the stroke line

  An active anchor point is solid (■)
  an inactive anchor point has a clear centre (□)

- Repeat the same process for **b, c** and **d**
  Each time the next anchor point is added, all other anchor points show as inactive

Step 38: Delete An Anchor Point

Delete Anchor Point Tool Hot Key **-**

- Select the **Delete Anchor Point Tool** Hot Key **-**
  The Hot Key - option works from both the second row of the keyboard and the number key pad
- Click onto the centre of the hem line **e** to delete the anchor point
- Deselect the **Delete Anchor Point Tool**

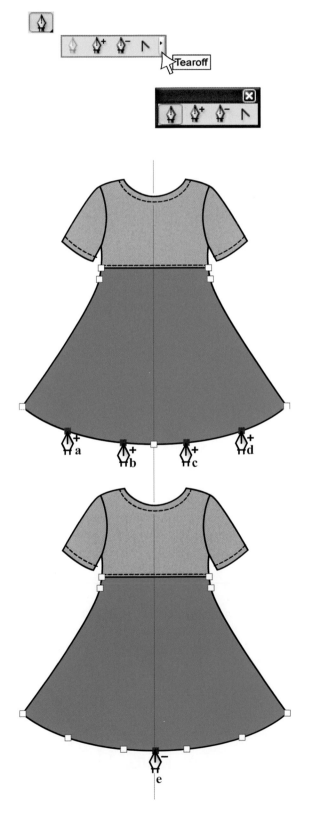

Click

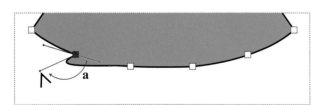

Click

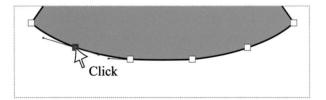

a

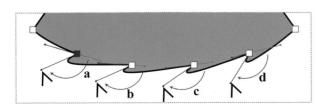

a
b
c
d

Zoom Tool Hot Key **Z**
Direct Selection Tool Hot Key **A**
Convert Anchor Point Tool Hot Key **Shift C**

- Marquee over the hemline with the **Zoom Tool** Hot Key **Z**
- Select the **Direct Selection Tool** Hot Key **A**
- Click onto the edge of the dress shape to highlight the anchor points

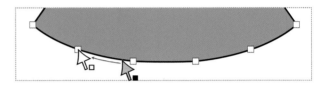

- Select the first anchor point by running the **Direct Selection Tool** Hot Key **A** along the hem line of the skirt until the black square next to the arrow turns clear

Click onto this **Anchor Point** to highlight the **Handles**

- Select the **Convert Anchor Point Tool** Hot Key **Shift C**
- Click onto the first **Anchor Point a** and drag the **Handle** as directed in the illustration
- Repeat the same procedure for **Anchor Points b, c** and **d**

- Zoom out Hot Key **Ctrl −** Apple OS **Cmd -**
- To zoom out gradually, hold Hot Key **Ctrl** or the Apple OS **Cmd** key down and tap the **subtraction** key until you have the view required

!REMEMBER!
Zoom For Det **ails**

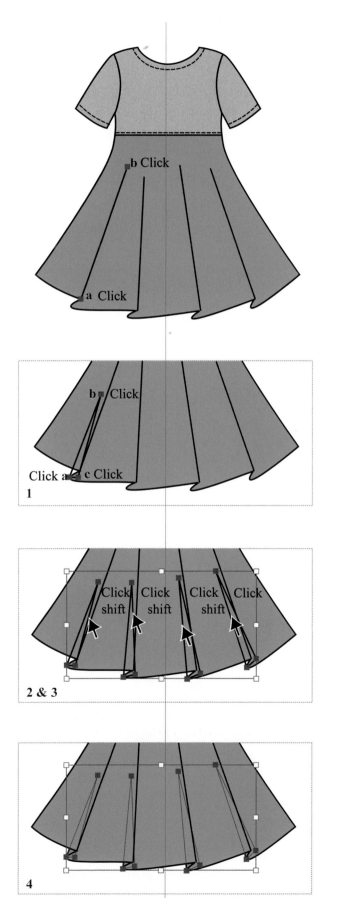

Pen Tool Hot Key **P**
Selection Tool Hot Key **V**

- Select the **Pen Tool** Hot Key **P**
- Click onto the first drape at the hem point **a**
  *Be careful not to click onto the stroke as this will add an **Anchor Point***
- Click again closer to the bodice **b**
- Click onto the **Selection Tool** Hot Key **V** to deselect the **Pen Tool**
- Repeat this process for the other three lines

Pen Tool Hot Key **P**
Selection Tool Hot Key **V**
Eye Dropper Hot Key **I**

- Create folds to go behind each drape using the drape line as a guide:
  1: Select the **Pen Tool** Hot Key **P**
  The stroke only has colour (⬚)
- Click onto the fold back of the drape **a**
- Click onto the skirt next to the drape line **b**
- Click to the right **c** and close the shape by clicking back onto **a**
  2: Repeat this process for all four drapes
  3: Select each fold back with the **Selection Tool** Hot Key **V** by clicking onto each shape, holding the **Shift** key down at the same time. Holding the **Shift** key down allows the selection of multiple objects at the same time
- Keeping all four shapes selected click onto the **Eye Dropper** Hot Key **I**
- Place the **Eye Dropper** (🖋) on the skirt to copy the **Fill** and **Stroke** colours to the selected fold back pieces (▣)
- Do *not* deselect

  4 - The four fold-back pieces are still selected and now need to go behind the skirt
- Right click the mouse and a pop up menu will appear
- Select **Arrange**
- Click onto **Send To Back**
  Hot Key **Shift Ctrl [** Apple OS **Shift Cmd [**

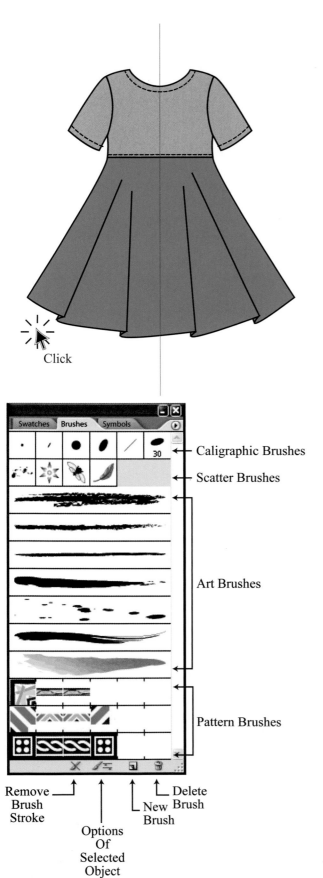

Click

Step 42: Group The Dress

Selection Tool Hot Key V

- Marquee over the whole dress with the **Selection Tool** Hot Key **V**
- Right click the mouse and a pop-up menu will appear
- Select **Group**
- Click away from the dress to deselect

Open Brush Stroke Palette:

- The **Brush Stroke** palette is used when a brush stroke is required - i.e. when depicting Twin Needle or Cover Stitch or any other fancy stitch details.

There are 4 options:

- **Calligraphic Brushes**: a Calligraphic Brush simulates the use of a calligraphic pen tip. This brush would be used when a more natural looking line is required when doing illustrations or drawings
- **Scatter Brushes**: a Scatter Brush scatters an object repeatedly along a path

- **Art Brushes**: an Art Brush stretches the design on a path between anchor points

- **Pattern Brushes**: a Pattern Brush repeats a pattern along a path from start to finish

Caligraphic Brushes

Scatter Brushes

Art Brushes

Pattern Brushes

Remove Brush Stroke

Options Of Selected Object

New Brush

Delete Brush

Step 43: Draw The Brush Stroke Repeat

Pen Tool Hot Key **P**
Selection Tool Hot Key **V**
Scissor Tool Hot Key **C**
Rectangle Tool Hot Key **M**

- Click onto the **Pen Tool** Hot Key **P**
- Draw a dashed line, following the dashed line instructions on page 39
- Deselect by clicking onto the **Selection Tool** Hot Key **V**
- Establish the horizontal repeat of the brush stroke, by dragging guide lines from the vertical ruler and placing one guide either side of the repeat
- Select the line with the **Selection Tool Hot Key V**
- Click onto the **Scissor Tool** Hot Key **C**
- Cut the overhang from the guide line of the dashed line by placing the cursor exactly on the blue line of the highlighted line and clicking, the overhang will be selected still and can be deleted by pressing the **Delete** key
- Select the line and hold down the **Alt** key, a double arrow will appear (➤), tap the down (↓) arrow on the keyboard
- Select the **Rectangle Tool** Hot Key **M**
- Place a colour into the fill box only (▣)
- Draw a rectangle over the repeat being careful to place the cursor exactly on top of the guide lines
- When the cursor rests on top of the guide line the vertical line of the cross will change colour
- Deselect the **Rectangle Tool** by clicking onto the **Selection Tool** Hot Key **V**
- Select the rectangle and send it to the back of the proposed brush stroke Hot Key **Shift Ctrl [**

- Remove the colour from the fill box (▢)
- There is now a transparent box at the back of the proposed brush stroke

- Select the whole object - the dashed lines and the transparent box - with the **Selection Tool** Hot Key **V**
- Click onto the **New Brush** icon (▣) in the **Brushes** palette

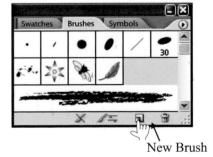

New Brush

!REMEMBER!
Zoom For Details +

53

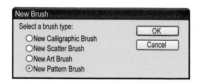

- Select **New Pattern Brush**
- Click onto **OK**

- A dialogue box will pop up with the brush in the first tile

- Leave the **Scale** at **100%** and the **Spacing** at **0%**

- Click onto **Stretch to fit (◉)**

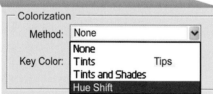

- Click onto the arrow to bring up the *"Colorization"* **Method** options
- Select **Hue Shift**
  Hue Shift: this will change the brush stroke colour whenever the stroke colour is changed - this method works best with a one colour brush stroke

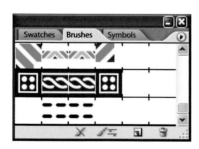

- Click **OK**
- The **New Brush** stroke is now in the **Brushes** palette

- Draw a line with a **1pt Stroke** and black in the stroke box (⬛)

- Click onto the **New Brush** stroke

- Change the colour of the **Brush stroke** by putting a new colour into the **Stroke** box (⬛)

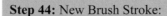

!REMEMBER!

Save the file Hot Key **Ctrl S** Apple OS **Cmd S**

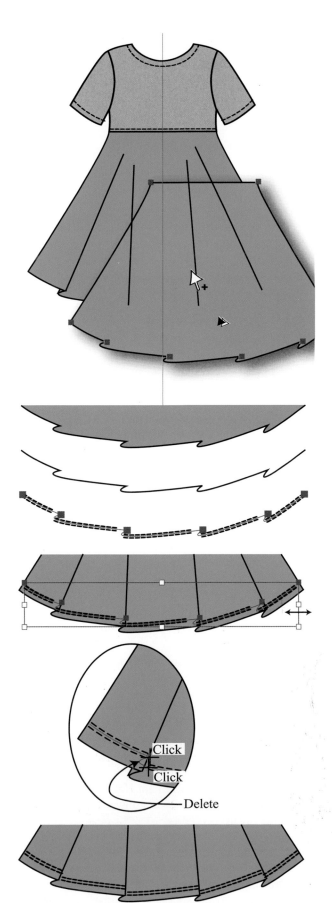

Step 45: Add The New Brush Stroke To The Dress.

Group Selection Tool No Hot Key
Direct Selection Tool Hot Key **A**
Scissor Tool Hot Key **C**

- Select the skirt with the **Group Selection Tool**
- Start to drag the skirt away and then press the **Alt** key to copy the skirt - it is important to drag the skirt completely clear of the original dress
- Click onto the **Direct Selection Tool** Hot Key **A** and marquee over the two waist **Anchor Points**

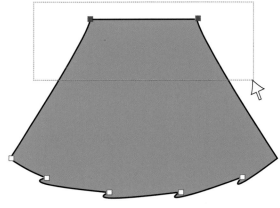

- **Delete** the selection
  The hem stitch line is still grouped with the dress
- Click onto the **Group Selection Tool** No Hot Key and select the hemline again
- Remove the fill from the hemline Hot Key **X** to bring the fill box forward (🔲)
- Do *not* deselect the hem line
- Click onto the new **2 Needle Top Stitch** brush
- Place the hem stitch line back onto the skirt
- Click onto the **Selection Tool** Hot Key **V** to reveal the bounding box and scale the hemline to fit onto the skirt
- Deselect
- Click onto the hem stitch line again with the **Group Selection Tool**
- Select the **Scissor Tool** Hot Key **C** and cut the hem stitch line, in line with the skirt folds
- Select the section between the cuts with the **Direct Selection Tool** Hot Key **A**
- **Delete** the selection

!REMEMBER!
Zoom For Det**ails**

CREATE A SIMPLE PATTERN FILL

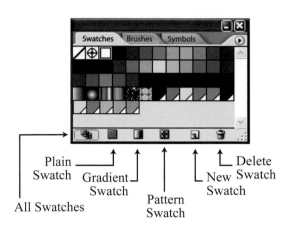

Plain Swatch
Gradient Swatch
All Swatches
Pattern Swatch
New Swatch
Delete Swatch

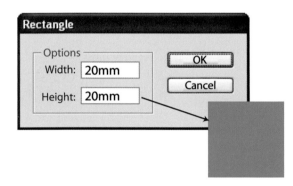

Rectangle

Options
Width: **20mm**
Height: **20mm**

OK
Cancel

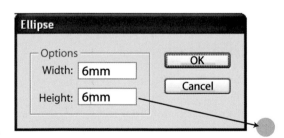

Ellipse

Options
Width: **6mm**
Height: **6mm**

OK
Cancel

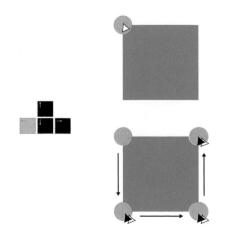

Open Swatches Palette:

- The swatch palette consists of three different kinds of swatches:

  Plain swatches: these are plain colour swatches

  Gradient swatches: a gradient is a gradual transition between two or more colours

  Pattern swatches: a swatch consisting of a repeat pattern

Step 46: Draw The Pattern Repeat

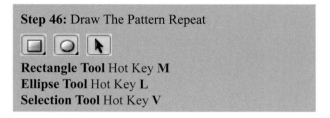

Rectangle Tool Hot Key **M**
Ellipse Tool Hot Key **L**
Selection Tool Hot Key **V**

- Select the **Rectangle Tool** Hot Key **M**
- Make sure there is only a **Fill** in the swatch box, not a **Stroke** (⬚)
- Click onto the work area to activate the **Rectangle** option box
- Type the size of the square, **20mm**, into the option box to create a 20mm square
- Deactivate the **Rectangle Tool** by clicking onto the **Selection Tool** Hot Key **V**
- Click Away

- Select another **Fill** colour for the spot (⬚)
- Select the **Ellipse Tool** Hot Key **L**
- Click onto the work area to activate the **Ellipse** option box
- Type the size of the circle into the option box
- There is now a **6mm** circle
- Deactivate the **Ellipse Tool** by clicking onto the **Selection Tool** Hot Key **V**
- Place the circle exactly on the corner of the square, the cursor will change to white when the centre of the circle is directly on top of the corner **Anchor Point**
- Set the **Keyboard** increment Hot Key Ctrl **K** Apple OS **Cmd K** at 20mm this will match the size of the square
- Select the spot, hold down the **Alt** key, a double arrow will appear (⇘), and tap the down (↓) direction key once to copy the spot to the next corner. Repeat the process to the right and up again
- This will copy the spot to each corner of the square

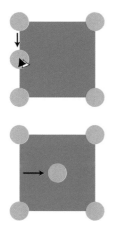

Step 47: Draw The Pattern Repeat Continued

Selection Tool Hot Key **V**

- Re-set the keyboard increment Hot Key **Ctrl K** Apple OS **Cmd K** to **10mm,** half the size of the square
- Select the top left spot and holding down the **Alt** key, tap the down direction key once
- Release the **Alt** key and tap the right direction key once

- This will copy the spot to the centre of the square

Step 48: Creating The Pattern Repeat

Selection Tool Hot Key **V**

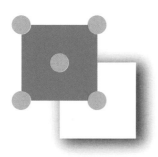

- Select the background square and copy it to the back of the shape Hot Key **Ctrl C; Ctrl B** Apple OS **Cmd C; Cmd B**
  Ctrl **C:** *"C" copies the shape*
  Ctrl **B:** *"B" represents the back or behind the object*
- Remove the fill colour from the copied square

  Tip: As the square is not visible, it would be useful to move the square out from behind the filled square, tapping the right direction key once, to check that the copied square has no fill in it. Once this is done, send the square back by tapping the left direction key once

- The repeat pattern swatch is now ready to go into the **Swatches** palette
- Marquee over the whole design with the **Selection Tool** Hot Key **V**

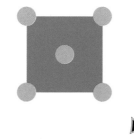

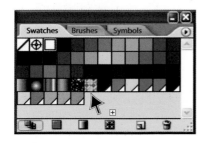

- Drag the selection into the **Swatches** palette

SCALING A PATTERN FILL

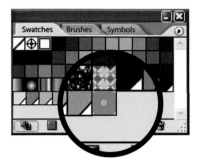

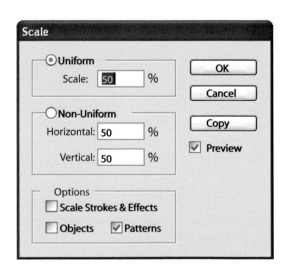

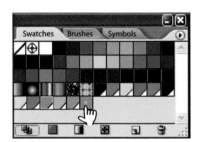

Step 49: Check The Pattern Repeat

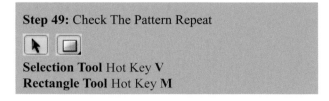

Selection Tool Hot Key **V**
Rectangle Tool Hot Key **M**

- The **New Pattern Swatch** is now in the **Swatches** palette
- Make sure that the **Fill** box is in front and click onto the **New Pattern** fill ( ). Check the repeat by drawing a **Rectangle** Hot Key **M**

Step 50: Scale The Pattern

- Select the rectangle with the pattern fill in it
- Right click the mouse - a pop-up menu will appear
- Select **Transform**
  ⟶ **Scale**
- An option box will appear
- Tick **Patterns** only - only the pattern not the object will be scaled
- Tick the **Preview** box - this will show a preview of the scale of the pattern, before the operation is accepted
- Select **Uniform**
- Type **50** in the **Scale** box

NEW LAYER, CHANGE THE COLOUR OF A GARMENT

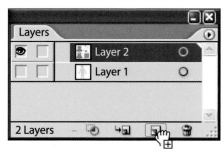

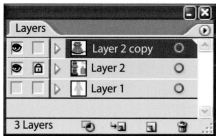

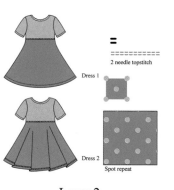

Layer 2   Layer 2 copy

Step 51: Make A Copy Of Layer 2

Selection Tool Hot Key **V**
Direct Selection Tool Hot Key **A**

- Make a copy of Layer 2 by dragging Layer 2 onto the **Create New Layer** icon ( )
- This will copy an exact replica of whatever was on Layer 2

- Lock and hide Layer 2 (👁 🔒) and click onto **Layer 2 copy**
- Select everything except the last dress completed and **Delete**
- Show Layer 2 by clicking onto the eye(👁)
  *Do not unlock **Layer 2***

- ***Layer 2:*** *will contain all the work done so far*

- ***Layer 2 copy:*** *will just have the latest dress in it*

- Click onto the **Direct Selection Tool** Hot Key **A**
- Select the *pink* bodice
- Go to **Select** in the menu bar
  → **Same** ⌐
          → **Fill Color**
  This will pick up all the pink in this layer
- Go the **Swatches** palette and click onto the new spot pattern swatch, this will now replace the pink

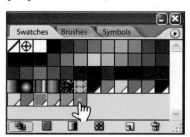

- Now select the blue in the same way and change that to the spot
  This will pick up all the blue in this layer

59

Dress 1

Dress 2

Spot repeat

Dress 3

Step 52: Scale The Pattern Fill

Selection Tool Hot Key **V**

- Select the spot pattern fill in the dress, using the **Select, Same Fill Color** method (refer to page 59)
- Right click the mouse - a pop-up menu will appear
- Select **Transform**
  $\longrightarrow$ **Scale**
- An option box will appear
- Tick **Patterns** only - only the pattern, not the object will be scaled
- Tick the **Preview** box - this will show a preview of the scale of the pattern, before the operation is accepted
- Select **Uniform**
- Type **50** in the **Scale** box (refer to page 58)

Step 53: Place All Dresses Within The Printable Area

Selection Tool Hot Key **V**

There should now be a series of dresses with various applications in the file. Some will no longer be in the **Artboard**

- To reveal the dotted lines that designate the **Printable Area,** click onto **View** in the menu bar
  $\downarrow$
  Show Page Tiling
- The dotted line will now be visible

- Unlock Layer 2
- Click onto the **Selection Tool** Hot Key **V**, as each of the dresses should be grouped they can now be picked up and placed within the **Printable Area**
- **Scale** the dresses to fit on the page as illustrated in the sketch, follow Step 50 and click onto **Objects** and **Patterns**
- Place the working drawing of the brush stroke and the pattern fill, with examples of each, on the page with the dresses

- Save the file Hot Key **Ctrl S**   Apple OS **Cmd S**

- Click onto **File** in the menu bar and go to **New**
  Hot Key **Ctrl N**   Apple OS **Cmd N**
  An option box will appear - do not name file
  Artboard Setup
  Select Size: A4
  Orientation: Portrait (**)**
  RGB Color (◉)
  OK
- Immediately save the file
  File
      Save As
          Local Disc C
             Illustrator Lessons
                Exercise 3 - B&W Dress
  This will save the file into the directory originally set up on page 4

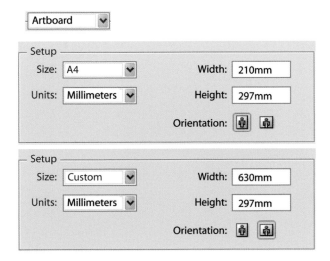

- Click onto **File** in the menu bar and go to
  Document Setup Hot Key **Alt Ctrl P** Apple OS
  Alt Cmd P
- The dialogue box should automatically open up on
  Artboard
- The present width of the Artboard is **210mm** - this
  is the width of an **A4** page in **Portrait**

- Multiply that width measurement by 3
  210mm × 3 = 630mm
- The Artboard setup will now show the size as
  Custom and the **Orientation** will be **Landscape**
- The Artboard is now big enough to hold three
  separate printable pages
- **OK**

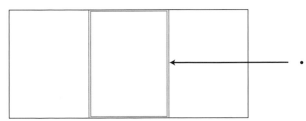

Note: different systems may look different to the illustration you see, What is important is the terminology
- Go to **View** in the menu bar
      Show Page Tiling

*There will only be one page in the centre of the **Artboard***

CREATE A NEW FILE WITH MULTIPLE PAGES

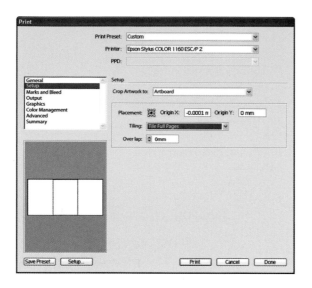

- Click onto **File** in the menu bar and go to
  Print Hot Key **Ctrl P** Apple OS **Cmd P**
- A dialogue box will appear and the default menu
  will be the **General** menu

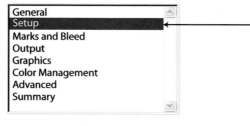

- Click onto **Setup**

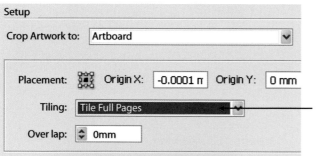

- This option will allow you to select:
  Tile Full Pages

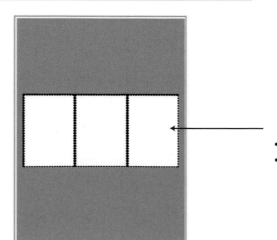

- This is the printable area view
- Click onto **Done**

Window

✓ Tools
Transform   Shift+F8
Transparency   Shift+Ctrl+F10
Type   ▶
Variables

Brush Libraries   ▶
Graphic Style Libraries   ▶
Swatch Libraries   ▶
Symbol Libraries   ▶

Illustrator lesson 1 (RGB Preview)
Exercise 2 - Dress (RGB Preview)
✓ Exercise 3 - B&W Dress (RGB Preview)

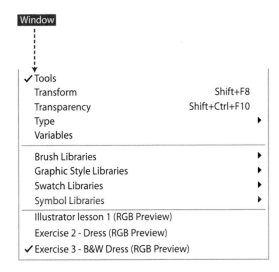

Dress 3

Step 4: Copy The Dress From Exercise 2 Into The New File

Selection Tool Hot Key **V**

- Click onto **Window** in the menu bar and go to the bottom of the menu. All the open files will be listed

- Click onto **Exercise 2 - Dress** to go back to that file

- Select the dress with the pattern fill and copy it
  Hot Key **Ctrl C** Apple OS **Cmd C**
- Go back to **Window** in the menu bar and select the new file - **Exercise 3 - B&W Dress**
- Once this file is open again, paste the dress
  Hot Key **Ctrl V** Apple OS **Cmd V**
  Save the file Hot Key **Ctrl S** Apple OS **Cmd S**

Step 5: Scale And Change The Colour Of The Dress

Selection Tool Hot Key **V**
Direct Selection Tool Hot Key **A**

- Select the dress with the **Selection Tool** Hot Key **V** and scale the dress to 185%
- Deselect the dress
- Click onto the **Direct Selection Tool** Hot Key **A** and select the spot fill
- Go to **Select** in the menu bar

      Same

            Fill Color
  This will pick up all the spot fill in the file
- Go to the **Swatches** palette and click onto white
- Deselect

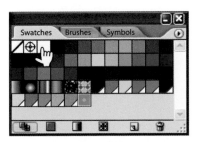

*Do not use the **Selection Tool** to select the dress, as this will select open paths (all the top stitch) and add fill to them*

Group Selection Tool No Hot Key

- Bring up the **Rulers** Hot Key **Ctrl R** Apple OS **Cmd R**
- Click onto the **Group Selection Tool** No Hot Key and select the front bodice
- Copy the bodice to the back
  Hot Key **Ctrl C** Apple OS **Cmd C**
  Hot Key **Ctrl B** Apple OS **Cmd B** copy to the back
- Do not deselect

- Go to the **Preferences** dialogue box Hot Key **Ctrl K** Apple OS **Cmd K** and set the keyboard increment to **5mm**

- Using the arrow keys on the keyboard, nudge the bodice out from behind the front bodice

- Change the colour of the bodice to light grey ( )

Step 7: Converting Front Neckline To Back Neckline

Zoom Tool Hot Key **Z**
Delete Anchor Point Tool Hot Key **-**
Group Selection Tool No Hot Key

- Zoom up to the bodice **Zoom Tool** Hot Key **Z**
- Click onto the **Delete Anchor Point Tool** Hot Key **-** and click onto the centre neck point to delete the anchor point
  Click onto the **Group Selection Tool**, select the back bodice and nudge it back into place with the down arrow on the keyboard

Step 8: Copy The Dress

Selection Tool Hot Key **V**

- Click onto the **Selection Tool** Hot Key **V,** select the dress and copy the whole dress by pressing the **Alt** key and dragging the dress to the second page
- Drag a vertical guide line out from the ruler and place it in the centre of the dress
- Deselect

Step 9: Converting Front Neck Stitch Line To Back Neck Stitch Line

Group Selection Tool No Hot Key
Direct Selection Tool Hot Key **A**

- Select the front bodice with the **Group Selection** No Hot Key **Tool** and **Delete** it
- Select the centre **Anchor Point** of the neck stitch line and drag up into position
- Select the back bodice and change the colour to white ( )

Step 10: Add Button Extension Overlap

Pen Tool Hot Key **P**
Eye Dropper Hot Key **I**
Selection Tool Hot Key **V**

- Select the **Pen Tool** Hot Key **P** and click onto the back bodice approximately **2mm** to the right of the centre guide line, not on the neckline as this will add an anchor point. Hold down the **Shift** key and move the cursor to the waist line, click again
- Change the keyboard increment back to 2mm and copy this new line to the left, by pressing the **Alt** key down and tap the left direction key, nudging the stitch line into place
- Do *not* deselect this line
- Select the **Eye dropper Tool** Hot Key **I**
- Place the eye dropper ( ) onto a dashed line - this will copy all the qualities of that line:
  Stroke size - 1
  Dashed Line - 3 (dash) and 2 (gap)
- Click onto the **Selection Tool** Hot Key **V, Deselec**t

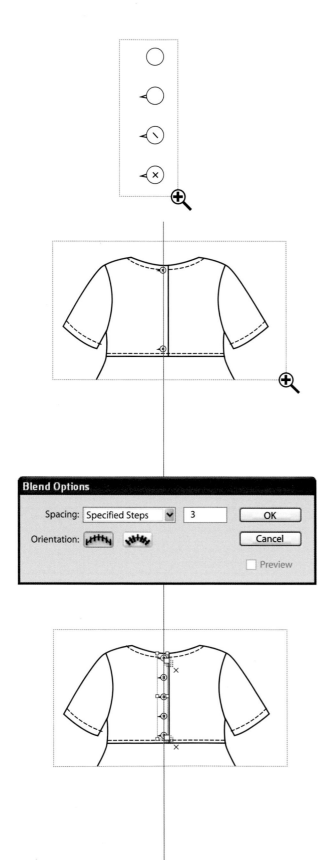

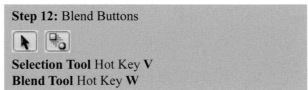

Step 11: Create Buttons

Ellipse Tool Hot Key **L**
Selection Tool Hot Key **V**
Pen Tool Hot Key **P**

- To continue, remove the tick (▣) from the dashed line box
- Select the **Ellipse Tool** Hot Key **L** and draw a circle by clicking onto the work area, holding down the **Shift** key to create a circle and drag the cursor to the size required
- Select the **Pen Tool** Hot Key **P** and draw the buttonhole next to the circle, deselect the **Pen Tool** by clicking onto the **Selection Tool** Hot Key **V**
- Re-select the **Pen Tool** Hot Key **P** and draw the centre stitch lines
- Deselect the **Pen Tool** by clicking onto the **Selection Tool** Hot Key **V**
- Marquee over the whole button and group it Hot Key **Ctrl G** Apple OS **Cmd G**
- Place one button at the centre back neck and copy and place another button at the centre back above the design line.
- Deselect

Step 12: Blend Buttons

Selection Tool Hot Key **V**
Blend Tool Hot Key **W**

- Double click the **Blend Tool** in the tool box and a dialogue box will appear
- In the **Spacing** option select **Specified Steps**
- Type **3** into the box next to **Spacing**
  This will place three buttons between the top and bottom buttons
- Select **OK**

- The **Blend Tool** is still selected, click once onto the top button and once onto the bottom button (⌨ₓ)
- Deselect

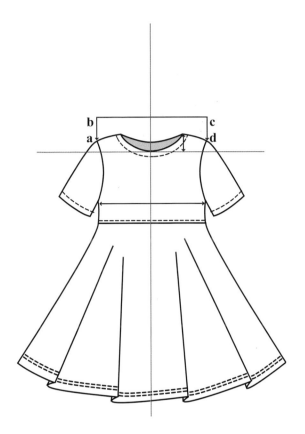

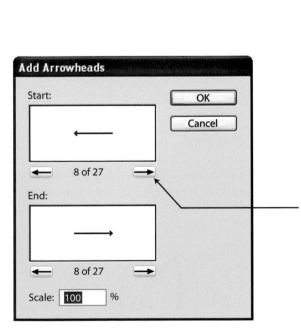

Step 13: Create Measuring Lines With Arrows

Pen Tool Hot Key **P**
Selection Tool Hot Key **V**

- Drag a guide line from the horizontal ruler to the centre of the front neckline
- Select the **Pen Tool** Hot Key **P,** click above the left shoulder point **a**
- Hold the **Shift** key down, move the cursor up and click again **b**
- Hold the **Shift** key down, move the cursor across to the right and click again **c**
- Hold the **Shift** key down, move the cursor down and click again **d**

If the lines you have just drawn do not align with the two shoulder points, select the lines with the Selection Tool Hot Key V and scale the selection until the lines align

Deselect the **Pen Tool** with the **Selection Tool** Hot Key **V** if you have not done so already

- Draw a line across the chest, making sure to leave enough space for the arrows
- Draw a line from the neck point to the horizontal guide line (for the front neck drop)
- Deselect the **Pen Tool** with the **Selection Tool** Hot Key **V**
- Select each of the lines with the **Selection Tool** Hot Key **V**, holding the **Shift** key down, so you can pick up the three separate lines at the same time

- Go to **Filter** in the menu bar
    ↓
  Stylize ─────┐
                    ↓
  Add Arrowheads

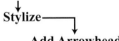

- A dialogue box will appear, you can now select the style of arrow, by clicking onto the arrows under the preview box - for this exercise we have selected arrow no: 8
- Select arrows for the start and end of the line
- **OK**

Step 14: Create A Circumference Measuring Line

Ellipse Tool Hot Key **L**
Scissor Tool Hot Key **C**
Selection Tool Hot Key **V**
Rotate Tool Hot Key **R**

- Select the **Ellipse Tool** Hot Key **L**
- Draw an ellipse using the skirt hem line as a guide for size
- Click onto the **Scissor Tool** Hot Key **C** and cut the ellipse either side of the skirt
- Select the section of the ellipse that goes over the skirt and **Delete** it
- Add the **Arrowheads** Hot Key **Shift Ctrl E** Apple OS **Shift Cmd E**
  *This Hot Key applies to the last operation performed in the **Effects** menu - in this case we had just used the **Add Arrowheads** effect*

- Add measuring lines to the back view

- Select the **Ellipse Tool** Hot Key **L**
- Draw an ellipse using the sleeve hem line as a guide for size, do not deselect
- Select the **Rotate Tool** Hot Key **R** and rotate the ellipse until it runs parallel to the sleeve hem
- Click onto the **Scissor Tool** Hot Key **C** and cut the ellipse either side of the sleeve

- Select the section of the ellipse that goes over the sleeve and **Delete** it
- Add the **Arrowheads** Hot Key **Shift Ctrl E** Apple OS **Shift Cmd E**
- Deselect

Dress - Style No: DR001
Front

a - Shoulder width
b - Chest circumference
c - front neck drop
d - Hem circumference

1

Dress - Style No: DR001
Back

e - Sleeve length from centre back to hem
f - Sleeve opening
g - Length from shoulder point to the waist
h - Back buttonstand width

2   3

Dress - Style No: DR001

3

Step 15: Place Front And Back Onto Separate Pages And Add Type

| T |

Type Tool Hot Key **T**

- Marquee over the front and group the measuring lines with the dress
- Repeat this process with the back and place the front and back on separate pages
- Select the **Type Tool** Hot Key **T** and click onto the work area where you want to place text
- Copy both the front and back onto page 3
- Scale the dress to 50% of the original size and type the style number above the dress

Step 16: Clear Guides

- Go to **View** in the Menu Bar
  ⟶ **Guides**
- A sub-menu will appear, select the **Clear Guides** option
- Save the file Hot Key **Ctrl S**   Apple OS **Cmd S**

- Copy the contents of page three Hot Key **Ctrl C** Apple OS **Cmd C**
- Create a **New File** Hot Key **Ctrl N** Apple OS **Cmd N**
- Paste the dress into this file Hot Key **Ctrl V** Apple OS **Cmd V**
- Do not save this file

- Export the file to a JPEG file

  JPEG image is a bitmap image that can be easily imported into other software

- Go to **File** in the menu bar

  Export

- The folder where all your work is saved will open

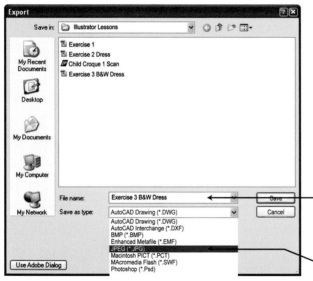

- Name the file: **Exercise 3 B&W Dress**
- In the **Save As Type** section click onto the down arrow to reveal the different file types the file can be saved as
- Select **JPEG(*.JPG)** - *this is the file extension*
- Click onto **Save**

- A Dialogue box with options will appear
- **Image Quality -** this has a direct impact on the file size and picture clarity
- **Color Mode -** this is the colour mode you are working in and will come up as the file colour mode

- **Resolution -** this is the DPI: this also has a direct impact on file size and clarity

- **Anti-Alias -** it is very important to tick **Anti-Alias,** as this will blur the edges of the line
  If this is not done, the drawing will be very unclear and "pixelated"

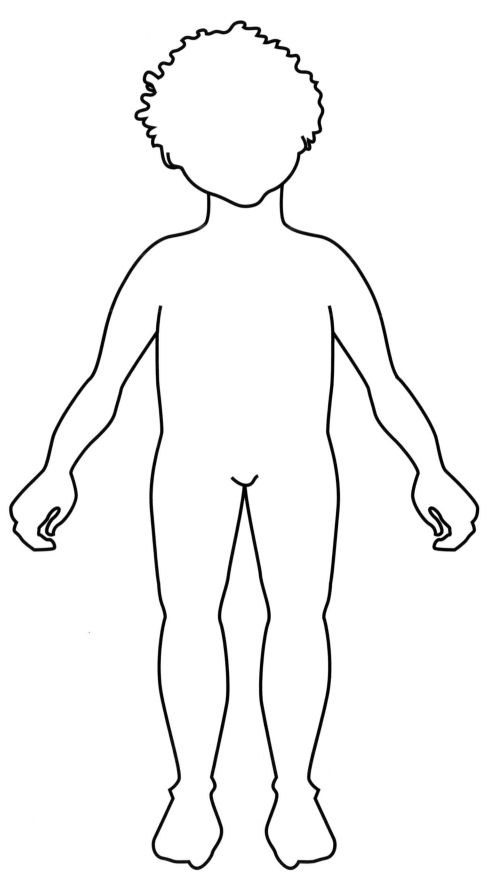

Child Croquis 1: Scan this image to use as a drawing template for the exercise in Chapter 2

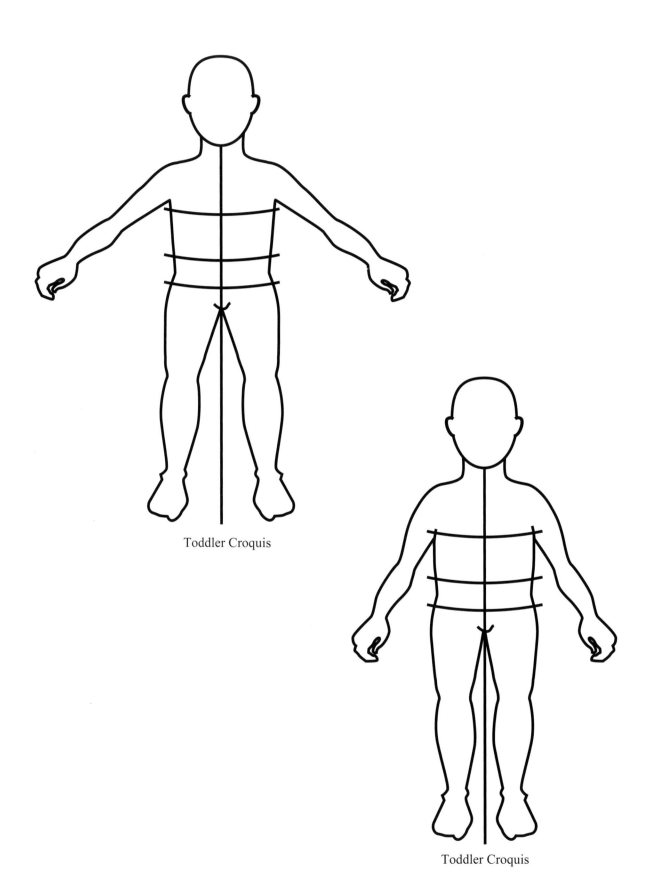

Toddler Croquis

Toddler Croquis

CHAPTER 3

TECHNICAL DRAWING

Technical Drawings And Trims

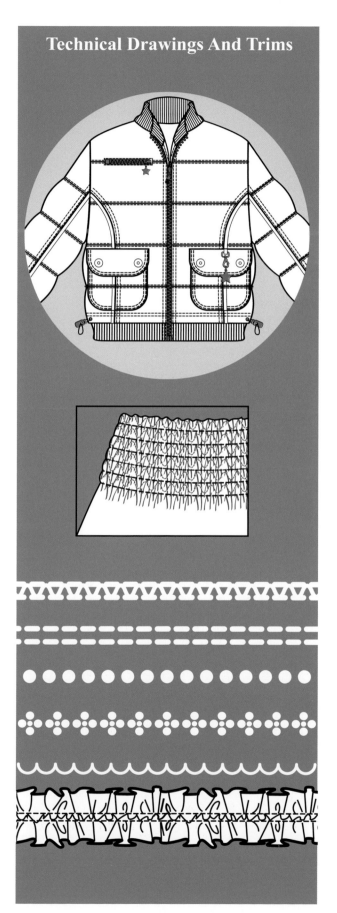

Chapter 3 combines the information learned in Chapters 1 and 2 to create detailed technical drawings for manufacturing. We also introduce the use of symbol and brush libraries to store different silhouettes, brushes and trims. We expand on the use of brush strokes introducing various stitch applications and the technical differences. The finished technical drawing is exported into JPEG format for importing into any spread sheet program.

CHAPTER 3

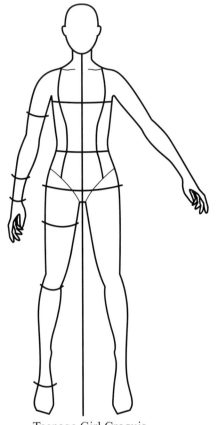

Teenage Girl Croquis

In this chapter we will build up a library of silhouettes and brush strokes that will allow ease and efficiency when creating technical drawings

Create Basic Silhouettes:

• Go to the last page in this chapter and scan in the Female Youth Croquis

• Create a series of basic silhouettes using the croquis as a guide
• Remember to create closed shapes
• Once the silhouettes have been drawn place them into the **Symbols** palette
*Symbols: A symbol is an art object that can be re-used in a document. Each symbol instance is linked to the symbol in the **Symbols** palette or a **Symbol** library. Using symbols can save time and greatly reduce file size. In this chapter we are using the symbols to create an easily retrieved library.*

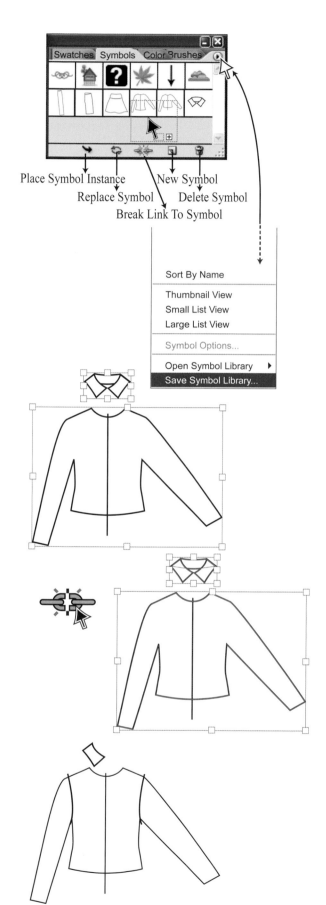

Place Symbol Instance

Replace Symbol

Break Link To Symbol

New Symbol

Delete Symbol

Sort By Name

Thumbnail View
Small List View
Large List View

Symbol Options...

Open Symbol Library ▶
Save Symbol Library...

Creating And Saving A Basic Silhouette Library:

- Placing an object into the **Symbols** palette is the same process as placing a **New Pattern Swatch** into the **Swatches** palette
- Select the silhouette you wish to place into the **Symbols** palette and drag it into the palette or click onto the **New Symbol** (⬛) icon
- Save this **Symbol Library** by clicking onto the option arrow just below the minimise/maximise/close icons
- A menu will appear with an option to save this Symbol Library
- Click onto **Save Symbol Library**
- Name the file - **Female Youth Silhouette Library** - so you can easily access it
- **Save**
- The file will now be located in the **Symbol Library** section of the program

Create A Denim Jacket Using A Basic Silhouette:

Selection Tool Hot Key **V**
Direct Selection Tool Hot Key **A**
Pen Tool Hot Key **P**

- Open a new file Hot Key **Ctrl N** Apple OS **Cmd N**
- Open the Silhouettes Library by clicking onto **Open Symbol Library** menu option from the **Symbols** options

- **Step 1:** Choose the jacket and collar silhouette from the **Female Youth Silhouette Library** palette (refer to page 74)
- For the jacket and collar to be edited it is important to click onto the **Break Link to Symbol** icon (⬚), this will make the silhouette into a vector image once again
- **Step 2:** Delete the back collar and the left front collar

- **Step 3:** Click onto the **Pen Tool** Hot Key **P** and ensure that there is only a stroke colour not a fill colour in the swatches (⬚), draw the armhole shape, extending beyond the silhouette as illustrated
- Reflect and copy the armhole shape and place it on the opposite side

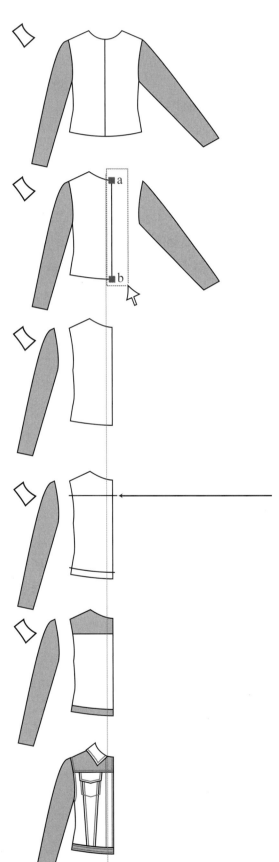

- **Step 4:** Marquee over the silhouette, armholes and the centre line with the **Selection Tool** Hot Key **V** and click onto **Divide** icon (⬚)
- Ungroup the jacket and drag a guide line to the centre line - make sure the guide line is locked

- **Step 5:** Delete the left half of the jacket leaving the left sleeve
- Marquee over the centre front neck point **a** and the centre front hem point **b** with the **Direct Selection Tool** Hot Key **A**
- Move these points to the right to create the button stand extension

- **Step 6:** Set the keyboard increment to **2mm** (refer to page 10)
- Select the right sleeve and move it aside with the direction keys on the keyboard - count how many times you move the sleeve: example three times or 6mm

- **Step 7:** Draw in the yoke and waistband seams, extending beyond the silhouette as illustrated

- **Step 8:** Marquee over the front jacket and the dividing lines with the **Selection Tool** Hot Key **V**
- Click onto the **Divide** icon (⬚) and divide the shape
- Three separate shapes have been created

- **Step 9:** Place the right front collar on the front jacket
- Draw all the style lines in black and the top stitch lines in grey, so that the lines are easily distinguished when applying the brush strokes

Step 10: Create Two Needle Top Stitch With A Corner:

Selection Tool Hot Key **V**
Direct Selection Tool Hot Key **A**
Rectangle Tool Hot Key **M**
Pen Tool Hot Key **P**
Scissor Tool Hot Key **C**
Rotate Tool Hot Key **R**
Group Selection Tool No Hot Key

*Creating a **Pattern Brush Stroke** with a corner tile is a slightly different process to one without a corner tile. In this instance we start with the repeat boundary box as the guide*

a: Draw a rectangle 1.25mm ✕ 2.5mm () (follow rectangle instructions on page 8 - open the option box to type in measurement)

b: Draw a dashed line **1pt** with a **Round Cap** (Follow dashed line instructions on page 39 - Dash: **2pt**, Gap: **1.5pt**) make sure there is only a stroke, not a fill in the **Stroke/Fill** boxes ()
- Cut off the line at the start of the second dash
- Centre the dash within the rectangle

c: Copy that line

d: Select the dashed lines and group them

Two Needle Top Stitch:

e: Marquee over the whole image and click onto the **Vertical Align Centre** icon in the **Align** palette ()

f: Set the keyboard increment to 1.25mm
- Click onto the top right hand corner of the rectangle with the **Direct Selection Tool** Hot Key **A** and move this to the right using the direction keys on the keyboard
- Repeat the same process for the bottom right corner

g: Set the keyboard increment to .625mm (half the size of the image) and move the stitches to the left
- Re-set the keyboard increment to 1.25 and copy the brushes twice more to the right and **Group** the image

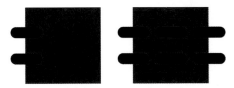

h: Copy the image and move that aside - this is the straight line part of the brush stroke
- Click onto the boundary box with the **Group Selection Tool** and remove the colour

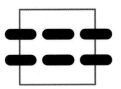

i: Copy the image again and rotate it 90° anti-clockwise

j: Align the two squares up next to each other
- vertically
*Note: when an object is selected and the cursor
is resting on an **Anchor Point** the **Selection Tool**
arrow will be black (▶), when placing that **Anchor
Point** directly on top of another **Anchor Point** the
Selection Tool arrow will turn white (▷) once the
two anchor points are aligned*

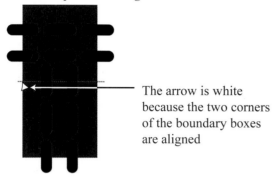

The arrow is white
because the two corners
of the boundary boxes
are aligned

k: Ungroup the whole image and delete the bottom
square and all other parts of the brush stroke until
the image that remains looks like the illustration

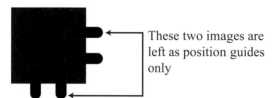

These two images are
left as position guides
only

l: Create the corner by copying a vertical stitch line
up to the corner

m: Draw a circle in the inner corner, using the inner
corner lines as guides
- Delete the guides and make the boundary box clear
- **The corner tile is complete**

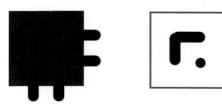

n: Drag the corner tile image into the **Swatches**
palette
- Double click onto the corner tile swatch to bring
up a dialogue box where you can name the swatch
- **Corner Tile**

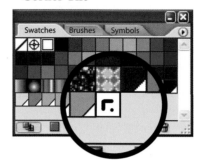

o: Select the straight line image and go to the
Brushes palette
- Click onto the **New Brush** icon (▧)
- Select **New Pattern Brush**
- Click onto **OK**
- A dialogue box will pop up with the brush in the
first tile
- Name the new stitch - **2 Needle Top Stitch**
- Click onto the next square **Outer Corner Tile**
- Select **Corner Tile** from the swatches listed in the
white box
- Click onto the next square **Outside Corner Tile**
and select the corner swatch again
- Leave the **Scale** at **100%** and the **Spacing** at **0%**
- Click onto **Stretch to fit** (◉)
- Click onto the arrow to bring up the *"Colorization"*
Method options
- Select **Hue Shift**
- **OK**

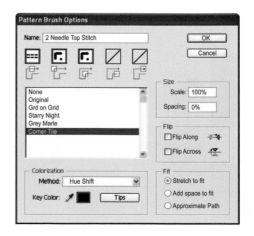

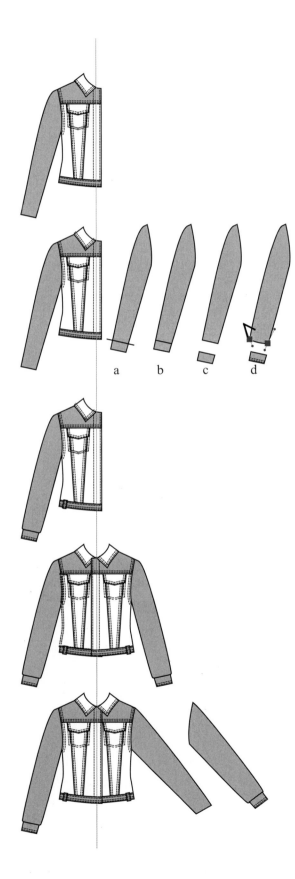

Create A Denim Jacket Using A Basic Silhouette Continued:

Selection Tool Hot Key **V**
Pen Tool Hot Key **P**
Ellipse Tool Hot Key **L**
Polygon Tool No Hot Key
Blend Tool Hot Key **W**

- **Step 11:** Select all the top stitch lines and click onto the new **2 Needle Top Stitch** you have just created
- Select the front button stand overlap lines and change them to dashed lines - use the same properties as the dashed line in Step 10:**b - 1 pt** stroke, Dash: **2pt**, Gap: **1.5pt** and a **Round Cap**
- Place the **2 Needle Top Stitch** onto the collar and group the collar and top stitch
- **Step 12:** Draw the cuff design line **a**
- Divide the sleeve with the cuff line **b**
- Ungroup the sleeve and cuff and move the cuff down with the direction keys on the keyboard **c**
- Draw a top stitch line on the cuff and manipulate the sleeve with the **Convert Anchor Point Tool** where the cuff is attached to the sleeve **d**
- Group the cuff and move it back into position
- Group the sleeve and cuff
- **Step 13:** Draw the belt loop onto the waistband
- Half the jacket is complete
- Marquee over the front of the jacket excluding the collar and sleeve and group the selection

- **Step 14:** Reflect and copy the front
- Start to move the front to the right and hold the **Shift** key down to keep the jacket in a straight line
- Send the new front to the back Hot Key **Shift Ctrl [** Apple OS **Shift Cmd [**

- **Step 15:** Delete the copied sleeve and move the left sleeve back into place and draw the design details as above

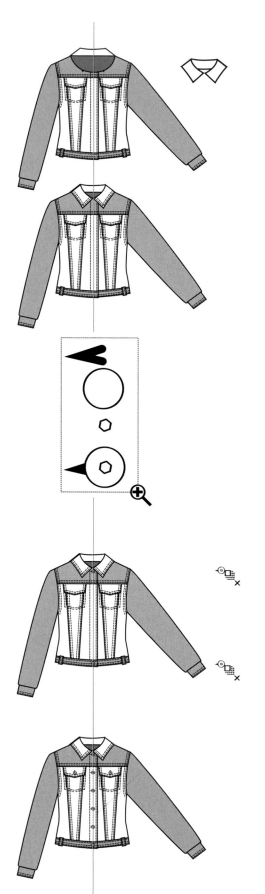

- **Step 16:** Create the back collar and back neck facing
- Select the collar from the symbols library and break the link (⬡)
- Draw in a half moon facing
- Select the back facing and back collar and send them to the back Hot Key **Shift Ctrl [** Apple OS **Shift Cmd [**

- **Step 17:** Create the buttons -
  a: Draw the buttonhole
  b: Draw an ellipse with the **Ellipse Tool** Hot Key **L**
  c: Draw a polygon with the **Polygon Tool** No Hot Key
  d: Place the polygon on top of the ellipse as the illustration and centre it with the **Align Tools** (⬡ and ⬡)
  e: Group the button and buttonhole

- **Step 18:** Place the button at the centre front neck
- Duplicate and place the last button at the hem
- Click onto the **Selection Tool** Hot Key **V** and select both buttons
- Click onto the **Blend Tool** Hot Key **W**
- Click onto the work area to activate the **Blend Tool** option box

- Select **Specified Steps** in spacing and type in **4** in the allocated space, click **OK**
- Click the **Blend Tool** onto the activated top button and hem button and the blend tool will create **four** buttons between the two activated buttons

- Place a button on each flap
- Marquee over the whole garment and group it

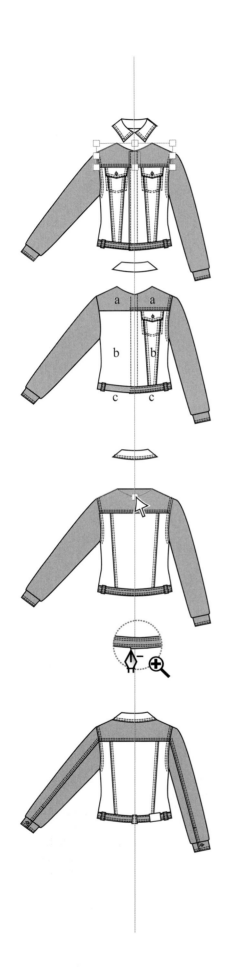

Denim Jacket: Back

Selection Tool Hot Key **V**
Direct Selection Tool Hot Key **A**
Delete Anchor Point Tool Hot Key **-**

- **Step 1:** Reflect and copy the front view
- Move the whole collar up using the keyboard direction keys
- **Step 2:** Click onto the **Selection Tool** Hot Key **V**, select the garment and ungroup it until the front yokes are able to be selected separately
- Using the Hot Keys is the easiest way to do this: **Shift Ctrl G** Apple OS **Shift Cmd G** to ungroup
- **Step 3:** Delete the front collar and leave the back collar
- Select both front yokes and join the shapes **a** together with the **Add To Shape Area Tool** in the **Pathfinder** palette () (refer to page 16)
- **Step 4:** Send the yoke shape to the back Hot Key **Shift Ctrl [** Apple OS **Shift Cmd [**
- Repeat this process for the back **b** and the back waistband **c**
- **Step 5:** Remove all the unnecessary details from this drawing, leaving only the two vertical style lines on the bodice
- **Step 6:** Average and join the yoke stitch lines and waistband stitch lines (refer to page 37)
- Draw in the stitch detail on the back collar and the armholes
- **Step 7:** Click onto the **Direct Selection Tool** Hot Key **A**, select the centre back neck anchor point and move it up to give the back neckline a better shape
- **Step 8:** Click onto the **Delete Anchor Point Tool** Hot Key **-** and delete any unnecessary anchor points

- **Step 9:** Group the back collar and move it back into place with the direction keys - if nothing has been moved and the keyboard increment is still the same, it should land exactly in the correct position
- **Step 10:** Draw in the style line details on the sleeves and cuffs and place the cuff buttons
- Draw the centre back belt loop

- **Step 11:** Draw a Rectangle to represent a leather badge
- Group the whole garment
  *Note: To copy style details from one side to the other remember to lock the rest of the garment down first - Hot Key **Ctrl 2** Apple OS **Cmd 2** - before selecting the details to copy*

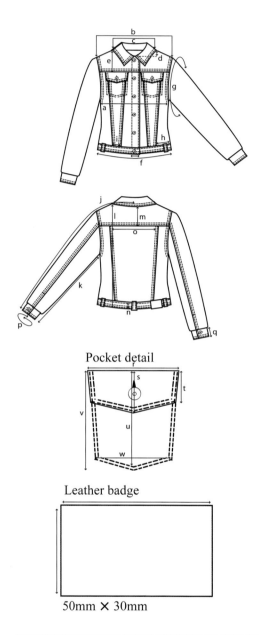

Pocket detail

Leather badge

50mm × 30mm

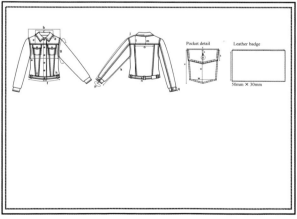

Denim Jacket: Measuring Points

Pen Tool Hot Key **P**

- **Step 1:** Click onto the **Pen Tool** Hot Key **P** and draw in all the measuring points (refer to page 67 - 68 for details)
- **Step 2:** Select the arrow heads for the measuring points
- Go to **Filter** in the menu bar

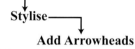

- A dialogue box will appear, you can now select the style of arrow, by clicking onto the arrows under the preview box - for this exercise we have selected arrow no: 8
- Select arrows for the start and end of the line
- **OK**

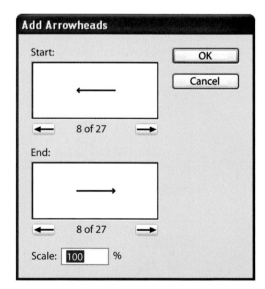

- **Step 4:** Draw in any details you want to highlight, like the pocket or the size of a badge

- **Step 5:** Type in all the **Points Of Measurement (POM)**

- **Step 6:** Arrange the garment on a page so that it will be compatible with the specification sheet you have set up
- In this example, the garment fits across half of the landscape orientation - see the example on page 83
- **Step 7:** Export the drawing to a JPEG file (refer to page 70)
- **Step 8:** Open up the program you create the specifications in and insert the JPEG file

Stray objects

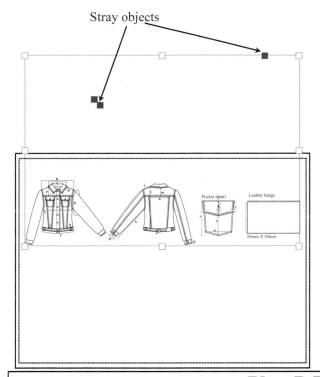

- It is important the only thing in the file that you are exporting is what you want to appear on the specification sheet
- The following points are how you can check your file:
  1. Check for **Stray Points** (refer page 37)
  2. **Select All** - go to **Select** in the menu bar

     All Hot Key **Ctrl A**
     Apple OS **Cmd A**

     Check that the **Bounding Box** is around the image to be exported only. If it is not, **Zoom Out** Hot Key **Ctrl −** Apple OS **Cmd −** and delete any other objects

  3. Note when exporting to a JPEG format quality and file size are associated - the higher the quality, the larger the file

Blu - D Design

Description: Denim Jacket	Size Range: 8 years to 14 years	Sample size: 12	Date: 05/05/2007

Pocket detail

Leather badge

50mm × 30mm

DESCRIPTION	POM	+/-	8	10	sample size 12	14			
CHEST 1CM BELOW UNDERARM	A								
SHOULDER BREADTH	B								
NECK WIDTH	C								
FRONT NECK DROP	D								
FRONT YOKE LENGTH	E								
HIP CIRCUMFERENCE	F								
HEM ARMHOLE	G								
SIDE PANEL WIDTH AT HIP	H								
POCKET PANEL WIDTH AT HEM	I								
SLEEVE LENGTH FROM NAPE OF NECK	J								
UNDERARM LENGTH	K								
TOTAL LENGTH FROM SIDE NECK	L								
CENTRE BACK YOKE LENGTH	M								
WAISTBAND WIDTH	N								
CENTRE BACK PANEL WIDTH	O								
TOTAL CUFF LENGTH (INC OVERLAP)	P								
CUFF WIDTH	Q								
POCKET FLAP WIDTH	R								
POCKET FLAP LENGTH - CENTRE	S								
POCKET FLAP LENGTH - SIDE	T								
POCKET LENGTH - CENTRE	U								
POCKET LENGTH - SIDE	V								
POCKET WIDTH - BOTTOM	W								

BRUSH STROKES

Brush Strokes:

- Following is a selection of useful brush strokes and instructions based on the two brush strokes you have already created
- The brush strokes are placed in an order where they build on each other

- Zig-Zag

- 2 Needle Cover Stitch

- 3 Needle Cover Stitch

- 1 × 1 Rib

- 2 × 2 Rib

- 3 × 2 Rib

Brush Strokes:

- Gathers

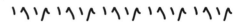

- Long Gathers

- Rouching

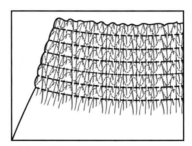

- Double Frill

- Spot

- Simple Lace

- Scallops

- Blanket Stitch

Brush Strokes:

- Chain Stitch

- Simple Zip   Realistic Zip

 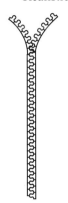

Drawing A Zig-Zag Line:

- **Size -** in a horizontal line, this will be the vertical height of the zig-zag
- **Ridges per segment -** this will be the amount of ridges on a **Path**/line between **Anchor Points**
- **Smooth -** the peaks of the zig-zag are rounded
- **Corner -** the peaks of the zig-zag are pointed

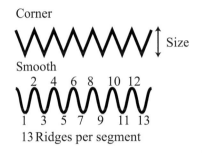

13 Ridges per segment

Drawing A Zig-Zag Line:

- **Step 1:** Draw a straight line

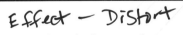

Effect – Distort

- **Step 2:** Go to **Filter** in the menu bar

  Distort
      Zig-Zag

- A dialogue box will appear in which you can select options
- Tick the preview option to check the zig-zag before accepting it

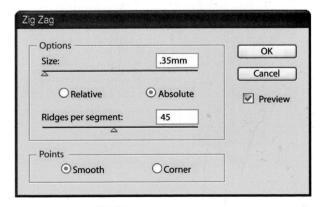

Creating A Zig-Zag Brush Stroke With A Corner:

- The reason you would use a zig-zag brush stroke as opposed to a zig-zag distorted line is because it creates an even distribution of the zig-zag regardless of the **Path**/line distance between **Anchor Points.** For example:

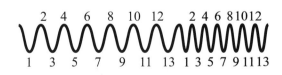

- The anchor point is not in the centre of the line, therefore the 13 ridges that are in the shorter part of the line seem relatively close. There is no way to change this in the palette
- The **Zig-Zag** distort is best used when there is an equal distance between anchor points along a path, as in a square or an ellipse

Create A Zig-Zag Stitch:

Selection Tool Hot Key **V**
Direct Selection Tool Hot Key **A**
Rectangle Tool Hot Key **M**
Pen Point Tool Hot Key **P**
Scissor Tool Hot Key **C**
Rotate Tool Hot Key **R**
Group Selection Tool No Hot Key

This brush stroke will be created using the same principles as the 2 × Needle Top Stitch with a corner

- **Step 1:** Draw a rectangle 1.25mm × 2.5mm ( ) (follow rectangle instructions on page 8 - open the option box to type in measurement)

- **Step 2:** Draw a line **.75pt** to fit within the rectangle and apply the **Zig-zag** (page 85) - keep the **Preview** box ticked to judge the size of the zig-zag, type in **1** ridge and select **Smooth**. Make sure there is only a stroke, not a fill in the **Stroke/Fill** boxes ( )

- **Step 3:** Align the edges of the zig-zag bounding box (the selected object highlight) with the boundary box

- **Step 4:** Marquee over the whole image and click onto the **Vertical Align Centre** icon in the **Align** palette ( )

Create A Zig-Zag Stitch:

ctl K

- **Step 5:** Set the keyboard increment to 1.25mm
- Click onto the top right hand corner of the rectangle with the **Direct Selection Tool** Hot Key **A** and move this to the right using the direction keys on the keyboard
- Repeat the same process for the bottom right corner

- **Step 6:** Set the keyboard increment to .625mm (half the size of the image) and move the stitches to the left
- Re-set the keyboard increment to 1.25 and copy the zig-zag twice more to the right and **Group** the image

- **Step 7:** Copy the image and move that aside - this is the straight line part of the brush stroke
- Click onto the boundary with the **Group Selection Tool** box and remove the colour

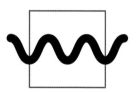

- **Step 8:** Copy the image again and rotate it 90° anti-clockwise
- Align the two squares up next to each other - vertically

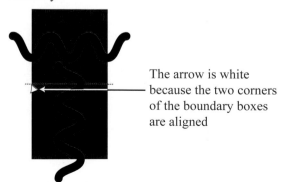

The arrow is white because the two corners of the boundary boxes are aligned

Create A Zig-Zag Stitch Continued:

- **Step 9:** Select the corner zig-zag
- Double click onto the **Rotate Tool** Hot Key **R** and type 45° into the Rotate option box or hold the **Shift** key down and rotate the corner zig-zag **45°** (refer to page 13)
- Move the zig-zag in towards the corner until it looks like the illustration

- **Step 10:** Delete the position guides

- Select the boundary box and make it transparent

- **Step 11:** Follow the instructions on page 78 to put the brush stroke into the **Brushes** palette

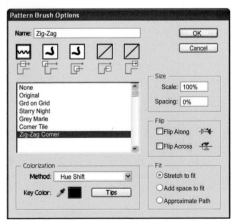

Create Two Needle Cover Stitch:

- The Two Needle Cover Stitch is a hybrid of the Two Needle Top Stitch (refer to pages 77-78) and the Zig-Zag you have just created

- **Step 1:** Select the Two Needle Top Stitch and the Zig-Zag brushes and drag them onto the work area

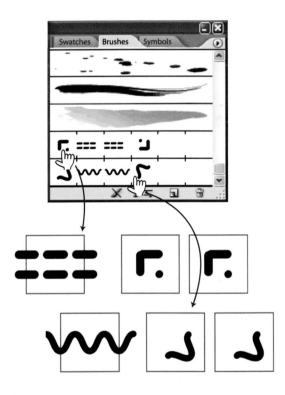

- **Step 2:** Ungroup the brushes and delete one of the corner tiles
- Place a stroke on the boundary boxes ( )
- Change the zig-zag to a red stroke( )
- Group each tile

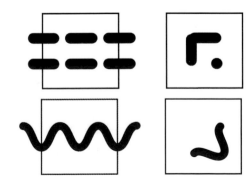

Create Two Needle Cover Stitch Continued:

- **Step 3:** Drag the Zig-Zag tiles directly on top of the Two Needle tiles - *note the arrow turns white when the two corner anchor points are on top of each other*

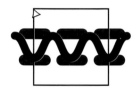

- **Step 4:** Delete the boundary box of the zig-zag

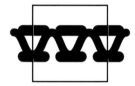

- **Step 5:** Remove the colour from the boundary box and () create the brush stroke

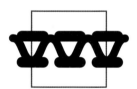

Create Three Needle Cover Stitch:

- **Step 1:** Copy a row of stitching into the centre of the Two Needle Cover Stitch and make it **.75pt**
- Follow the same process with the corner tile, creating a corner stitch line

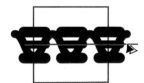

- **Step 2:** Create the Brush Stroke

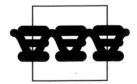

Create A 1 × 1 Rib:

- **Step 1:** Draw a vertical line - **1pt** and the length you require

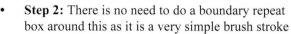

- **Step 2:** There is no need to do a boundary repeat box around this as it is a very simple brush stroke
- Select the line and create a new brush stroke
- Follow all the same instructions as other brush strokes except the **Spacing.** Make this 75%

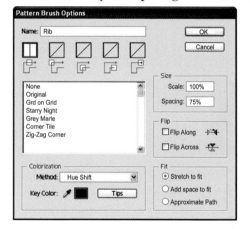

Create A 2 × 2 Rib and 3 × 2 Rib:

- These two rib variations are done the same way as the original brush stroke instructions with the repeat boundary box and the **Spacing** set at 0%

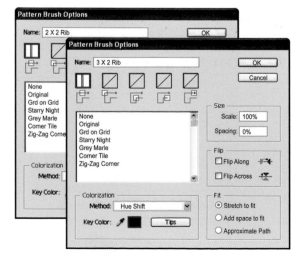

Create A Gathering Brush:

- **Step 1:** Click onto the **Pen Tool** Hot Key **P** and draw a series of gathers

- **Step 2:** Copy the gathers to the right to create a repeat
- Draw the repeat box using the copied gathers as a guide for the repeat

- **Step 3:** Create the Brush Stroke

Create A Gathering Brush Using A Calligraphy Brush From The Default Library:

- **Step 1:** Select the original Gathers brush stroke art work and manipulate the length by resting the cursor on the bottom centre anchor point until an arrow appears (↕) and drag the cursor down to lengthen the gathers

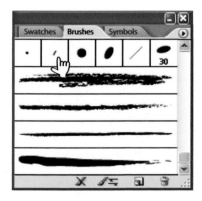

- **Step 2:** Select the gathers only, not the boundary box, and click onto a **Calligraphic Brush**

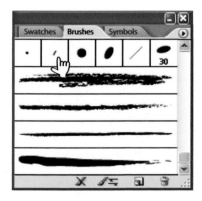

- **Step 3:** Create the brush stroke

Create Rouching Combining Different Brush Strokes: Dashed Line, Gathers and Zig-Zag Brush

- **Step 1:** Draw a **Dashed Line 1pt** with a **Round Cap**
- (Follow Dashed Line instructions on page 39 - Dash: **2pt**, Gap: **1.5pt**). Make sure there is only a stroke, not a fill in the **Stroke/Fill** boxes (▨)

- **Step 2:** Copy that line using the direction keys and set the keyboard increment to **1mm** and change the weight to **.75pt**, make the line solid not dashed
- Select the two lines and copy them twice more

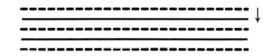

- **Step 3:** Change the solid line to the Gathered Brush stroke and adjust the stroke size until the proportion of the brush looks correct

- **Step 4:** Copy the Gathered Brush lines in front of the existing line Hot Key **Ctrl C, Ctrl F** Apple OS **Cmd C, Cmd F**
- Do not deselect the lines
- Select the Zig-Zag brush stroke and change the colour (▨)

- **Step 5:** Convert the Zig-Zag brush stroke to outlines
- Go to **Object** in the menu bar

Expand Appearance

You can convert brush strokes into the original paths in order to edit the individual components of the brushed line. Illustrator places the components of the expanded path into a group.

- Tick the dashed line option to give the Zig-Zag the appearance of an embroidered stitch line

DOUBLE FRILL

Create A Double Frill With A Colour In The Background:

- *To achieve the non-uniform effect of this brush stroke it is easier to hand draw the frill first and then scan it into Adobe Illustrator*

- **Step 1:** Lock the scanned image down
  Hot Key **Ctrl 2** Apple OS **Cmd 2**
  and draw over the top of the frill, the longer the repeat the less uniform the frill

- **Step 2:** Copy the frill repeat to the right
- Click onto the **Direct Selection Tool** Hot Key **A** and align the lines of the first repeat with the second repeat. Delete the second repeat once this is done

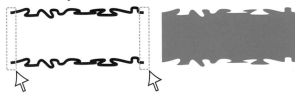

- **Step 3:** Copy the frill repeat
- Marquee over the anchor points on either end with the **Direct Selection Tool** Hot Key **A**
- Join the anchor points and put a fill (⬛) only into this shape

- **Step 4:** Place the line drawing of the frill on top of the solid colour. Draw the centre stitch lines and gathers with the **Pen Tool** Hot Key **P**

- **Step 5:** Draw the repeat boundary box and create the brush stroke

Change The Background Colour Of The Double Frill:

- **Step 6:** This brush stroke has a colour in it, therefore the way of saving the brush will have one difference: in the **Colorization** option next to **Method** the choice must be left at **None**
- Changing the colour of this brush stroke will require dragging the brush stroke out of the palette, changing the colour and re-creating the brush stroke

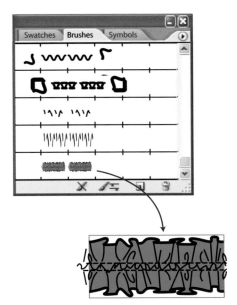

- Double frill placed in a shirt

- The same principles can be applied to any brush stroke

Create A Spot Brush Stroke:

- **Step 1:** Click onto the **Ellipse Tool** Hot Key **L** and draw a circle

- **Step 2:** There is no need to do a boundary repeat box around this as it is a very simple brush stroke
- Select the circle and create a new brush stroke
- Follow all the same instructions as other brush strokes except the **Spacing -** make this 50%

Create A Simple Lace Brush Stroke:

- **Step 1:** Draw a circle and create a simple pattern

- **Step 2:** Select the **Rectangle Tool** Hot Key **M** and draw the boundary box over the repeat

- **Step 3:** Create the brush stroke

Create A Scallop Edge Brush Stroke:

- **Step 1:** Draw a circle and delete the top anchor point

- **Step 2:** Select the **Rectangle Tool** Hot Key **M** and draw the boundary box over the repeat

- **Step 3:** Create the brush stroke

Create A Blanket Stitch Brush Stroke:

- **Step 1:** Click onto the **Rectangle Tool** Hot key **M** and create a **2.5mm** square
- Select the **Ellipse Tool** Hot Key **L** and draw a **2mm** circle

- **Step 2:** Delete the bottom and side anchor points and align the quarter of a circle with the side of the square
- Reflect and copy this to the opposite side
- Marquee over the two centre anchor points, making sure not to select the square, and average the two

- **Step 3:** Finish off the pattern by drawing a loop with one pointed edge and one rounded edge
- Copy this tile and remove the colour in the repeat boundary box

- **Step 4:** Set the keyboard increment to 2.5mm and copy the tile once to the right and once to the bottom
- Rotate the bottom tile 90° anti-clockwise

- **Step 5:** Move the loop aside and rotate it 45°
- Rotate the left quarter circle 90° anti-clockwise and align it with the bottom tile

- **Step 6:** Move the loop back into place and delete the tiles either side of the corner tile
- Remove the colour from the repeat boundary box

- **Step 7:** Create the brush stroke with a corner tile (refer to the Two Needle Top Stitch brush stroke)

Create A Chain Stitch Brush Stroke:

- **Step 1:** Click onto the **Pen Tool** Hot Key **P** and **d**raw a Chain Stitch link
- Copy a second link to the right to establish the repeat

- **Step 2:** Draw the repeat boundary box

- **Step 3:** Create the brush stroke

Create A Simple Zip Brush Stroke:

- **Step 1:** Draw a short vertical line **2pt** thick

- **Step 2:** There is no need to do a boundary repeat box
- Select the line and create a new brush stroke
- Follow all the same instructions as other brush strokes except the **Spacing** - make this 50%
- You can offset and overlap the two sides of the zip slightly to make it more realistic

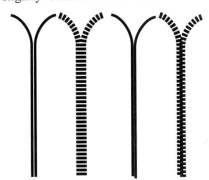

Create A Realistic Zip Brush Stroke:

This zip would be used for a prominent zip detail. It comprises of two sides and a centre brush stroke, that is three brush strokes

Side 1 Side 2   Closed zip

Create A Realistic Zip Brush Stroke:

- **Side 1, Step 1:** Click onto the **Pen Tool** Hot Key **P** and draw half a zip tooth ( )
- Reflect and copy the half tooth and join it to make a full shape

- **Step 2:** Draw the repeat boundary box

- **Step 3:** Create the brush stroke

- **Side 2, Step 1:** Rotate the zip tooth 180° and create another brush stroke

*The reason we create two separate brush strokes is because this brush has a notable right side up and if a line with the **Open Zip Side 1** is reflected the brush stroke will be incorrect - see illustration **a**. The illustration with the **Open Zip Side 2** is illustrated in **b***

a   b

- **Closed Zip, Step 1:** Place two copies of **Side 2** next to each other and one copy of **Side 1** in the centre as the illustration

- **Step 2:** Draw the repeat boundary box

- **Step 3:** Create the brush stroke

Save A Brush Stroke Library:

You now have the start of a good basic **Brush Stroke Library**. You can save this library so that it is easily accessible in any other file and you can add to it as well

- **Step 1:** Save the file as an a.i (Adobe Illustrator) file with a path you can easily find again
- **Step 2:** Save the **Brush Library** by clicking onto the option arrow just below the minimise/maximise/close icons

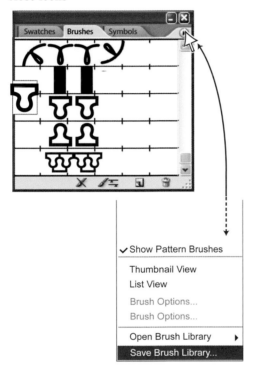

- A menu will appear with an option to save this Brush Library
- Click onto **Save Brush Library**
- Name the file - **General Brush Strokes Library** - so you can easily access it
- **Save**
- The file will now be located in the **Symbol Library** section of the program
- To re-access the library click onto the arrow again and go to **Open Brush Library**

  └──→ **Other Library**

- A file directory will open and you will be able to select the library you have created
- To embed the brush strokes into the file you are working on you just need to click onto the brush you require

Create A File Of Useful Accessories:

The following are some ideas of garment trims and accessories that have been created and filed in a Symbol Library. The accessories were created either by drawing over scanned accessories or by downloading accessory ranges from the Internet

Zip pull variations

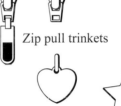

Zip pull trinkets

Cord locks   Cord Ends

Overall buckle   Dog clip
and slide adjuster

- Save this Symbol Library as you did the brush strokes

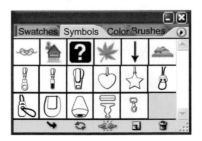

MASKING - RIB NECKBAND

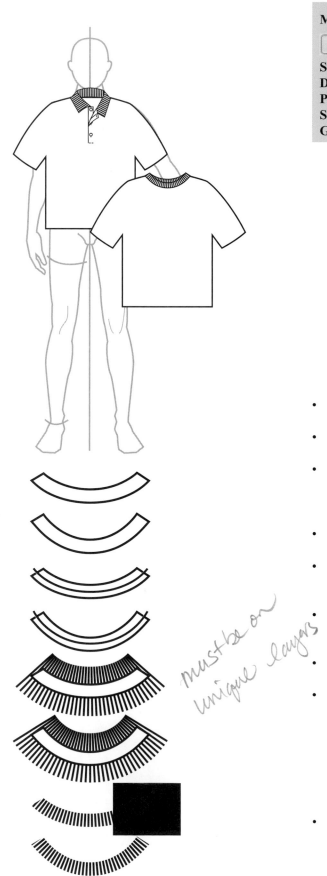

It would also be useful to keep a library of common garment pieces that you will use often. A rib neckband, a polo collar or a business shirt collar. The following information will demonstrate how to create rib trims using the **Clipping Mask**

Clipping Mask - a Clipping Mask works like a frame containing the objects within the confines of the masking shape. A mask can only be a vector image, bitmap and vector images can be masked. ***When an image is masked all the objects within the mask are grouped***

- Create a basic short sleeve tee shirt shape on the male youth croquis
- Draw in the shape of the rib neck band - front and back
- Copy the neckbands and move them away from the tee shirt shape (keep the original neckbands as reference) Hot Key **Ctrl C, Ctrl V** Apple OS **Cmd C, Cmd V**
- Click onto the **Pen Tool** Hot Key **P** and draw a line through the centre of each neck band
- Select both lines, go to the **General Brush Strokes** Library you have created and select the 1 ✕ 1 Rib brush
- Select the rib line on each neckband and **Send Them To The Back** Hot Key **Shift Ctrl [** Apple OS **Shift Cmd [**
- Select the rib and the rib neckband shape and **Make A Clipping Mask**
- Go to **Object** in the Menu Bar
  ↓
     Clipping Mask⌐
                Make
                Hot Key **Ctrl 7** Apple OS **Cmd 7**

- Once the **Clipping Mask** has been made, the original shape that you masked with will become transparent - note the red square in the illustration

must be on unique layers

Masking A Rib Neckband And Collar Continued:

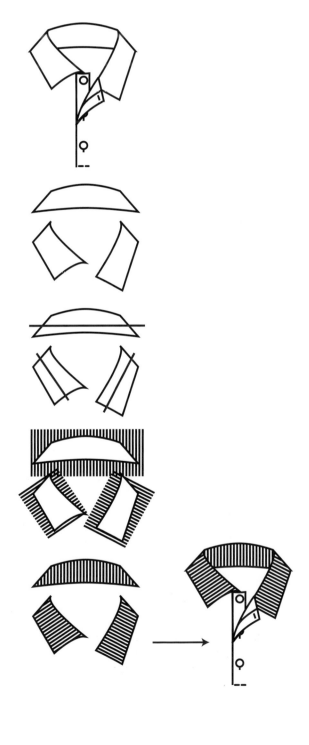

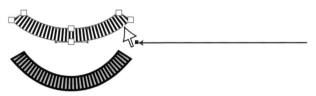

- Click onto the edge of the transparent neckband shape with the **Direct Selection Tool** Hot Key **A**
- The way to determine that the **Direct Selection Tool** is resting on the edge of the shape is by the appearance of a black square, when this occurs you can select the shape and put the **Fill** and **Stroke** in (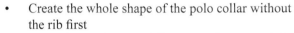)

- Create the whole shape of the polo collar without the rib first
  Tip: When a shape is difficult to achieve it is helpful to draw the shape over a photograph, or if you find it easier, hand draw the shape, scan it in and draw over the top of it.

- Copy the collar shapes and move them away from the tee shirt shape (keep the original collar as reference) Hot Key **Ctrl C, Ctrl V**   Apple OS **Cmd C, Cmd V**
- Click onto the **Pen Tool** Hot Key **P** and draw a line through the centre of each collar shape
- Select all the lines, go to the **General Brush Strokes Library** you have created and select the 1 ✕ 1 Rib brush
- Select the rib line on each collar shape and **Send Them To The Back** Hot Key **Shift Ctrl [** Apple OS **Shift Cmd [**
- Select the rib and the collar shape and **Make A Clipping Mask**
- Go to **Object** in the Menu Bar
  ↓
  Clipping Mask⌐
         ↓
     Make
      Hot Key **Ctrl 7** Apple OS **Cmd 7**
Or
Hot Key **Shift Ctrl 7** Apple OS **Shift Cmd 7**, to release a Clipping Mask

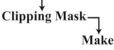

*Note: A **Mask** cannot be made with more than one shape at a time - that is: you cannot select the three collar shapes and **Make A Clipping Mask** in one operation - each shape must be selected and masked. However, you can mask as many shapes as you need to*

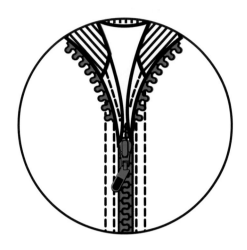

Expanding Brush Strokes And Symbol Trims:

- The zip brush was created with no fill in each tooth
- This zip front was created by expanding the zip brush (refer to page 89)
- The zip pull is a symbol from the **Trim Library**
- It has been expanded so that it can be manipulated and have colour added

- Zip pull with trinket

- Dog clip with trinket

- Cord lock

- Completed jacket

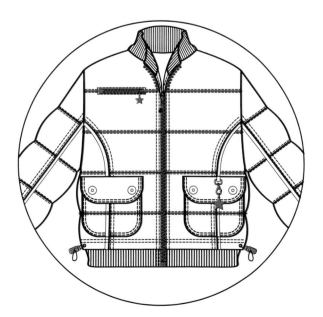

Create Style Symbols:

- You can scan the croquis on page 99 to create a library of basic style shapes - here are a few examples
- The detail or lack of detail are a personal choice

Single breasted long line jacket

Single breasted short jacket

Knit top

Knit roll collar

Knit V neck

Basic tee shirt

Basic shirt

Denim jacket

Tailored wide trousers

Pencil skirt

Short flared skirt

Skinny jeans

MALE GARMENT SYMBOLS

Create Style Symbols:

- The style symbols you create will be determined by the nature of the work you most commonly do

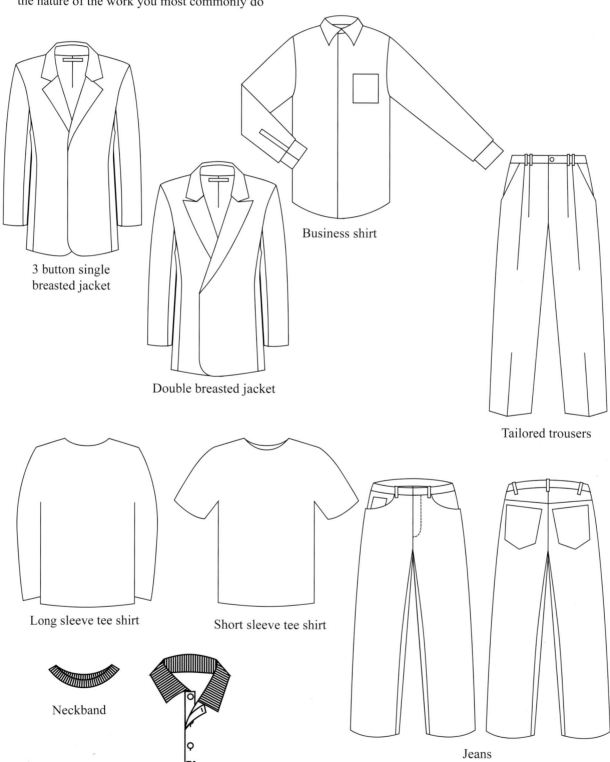

3 button single breasted jacket

Double breasted jacket

Business shirt

Tailored trousers

Long sleeve tee shirt

Short sleeve tee shirt

Neckband

Polo collar

Jeans

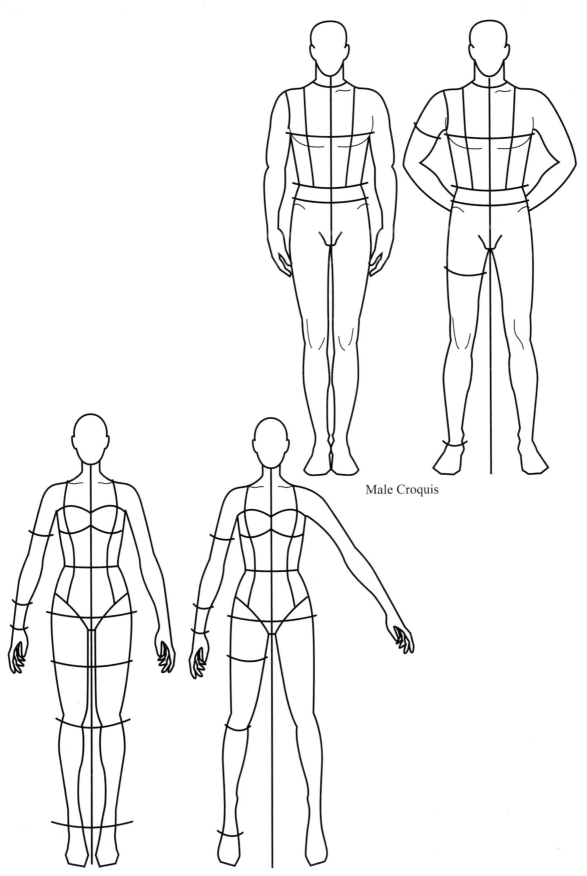

Male Croquis

Female Croquis

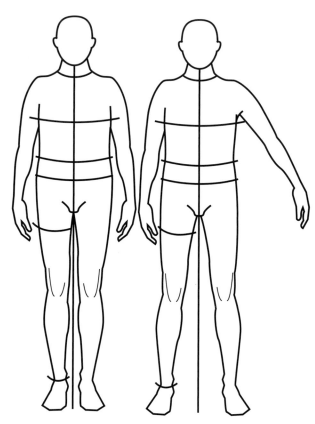

Male Youth Croquis

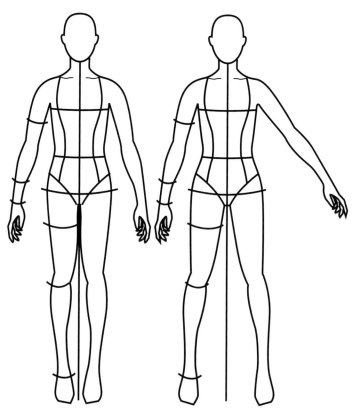

Female Youth Croquis

CHAPTER 4

STORY BOARDS

Chapter 4 introduces story boards using a mixture of scanned images, digital photographs and Adobe Illustrator drawings. We also introduce you to creating a pattern fill out of a scanned fabric and more complex pattern repeats and brush strokes. The illustration style is based on clean technical drawings. The unique components in each garment are demonstrated.

First Story Board

Spring into summer in the freshest of blue

The final product in Chapter 4 is a story board made up of garments containing a variety of brush strokes, pattern fills, scanned images, badges, labels and logo buttons.

The structure of this chapter will take you through the details of the pattern fills, brush strokes and accessories in each garment, style by style. We will not be giving you instructions on how to draw the garment as the principles covered in Chapter 1 and Chapter 2 have covered this. We will start with the simplest style and build up increasingly to more complex styles. We will include bitmap images as well as using type in the context of a story board.

Rib Top - Components:

1. **Scanned grey marle fabric or plain fabric swatch**

2. **Twin Needle stitching**

3. **Binding**

5. **Bead trim around neck**

- Create a **New File** and save this into your original folder

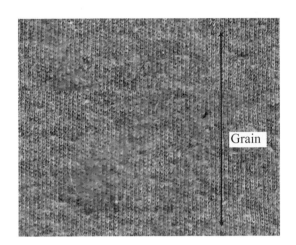

Grain

Scan A Plain Fabric:

- Scan in an actual piece of grey marle or plain fabric and save as a JPEG or TIFF file onto your
  C Drive ───────────┐
      📁 **Adobe Illustrator Exercises**───────┐
                           Grey Marle Scan

- Please note all scanners are different and there are two points to consider:
  1) Scan the image at 200 DPI (Dots Per Inch)
  2) Scan this image in colour
  For all other instructions follow the scanner instructions
- If your scanner allows, crop the image to about 10cm ✕ 10cm before scanning
  It is important to watch that you place the grain of the fabric parallel with the edge of the scanner - see the grain in the illustration

Create A Pattern Fill From The Grey Marle Fabric:

Selection Tool Hot Key **V**
Rectangle Tool Hot Key **M**

- Create and save a **New File** Hot Key **Ctrl N** Apple OS **Cmd N**
- Go to **File** in the menu bar, **Save As**, name the file - "**Story board Girls 8-14 years**"
- Open the file with the Grey Marle Scan and select and copy the swatch Hot Key **Ctrl C** Apple OS **Cmd C**
- Go to **Window** in the menu bar, scroll down to the end. Click onto **Story Board Girls 8-14 years** and paste the swatch into this file Hot Key **Ctrl V** Apple OS **Cmd V**
- Draw a square with the **Rectangle Tool** Hot Key **M** over the top of the grey marle or plain fabric swatch
- Do not deselect
- Send the square to the back of the swatch Hot Key **Shift Ctrl [** Apple OS **Shift Cmd [**
- Do not deselect
- Remove the colour from the square Hot Key / (📇)
- Click onto the **Selection Tool** Hot Key **V,** deselect by clicking away
- Marquee over the swatch and the transparent square behind the swatch and drag this into the **Swatches** palette
- Click onto the top and fill it with the scanned fabric

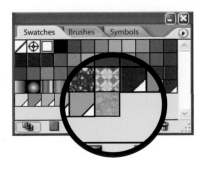

Refer to page 57 - A simple pattern fill

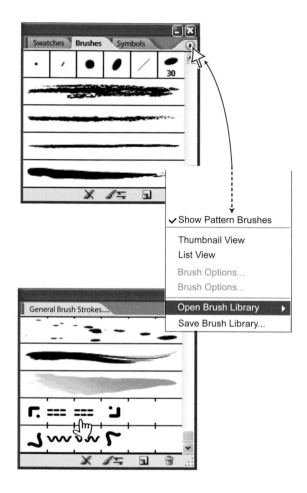

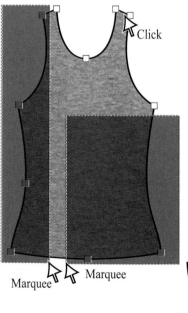

2 Needle Top Stitch: Open The Library Created In Chapter 3

- To retrieve a brush stroke created in another file, follow these steps:
- Go to **Window** in the Menu Bar
                    ↓
          Brush Libraries ─────┐
                                    ↓
              Other Libraries
- The file directory will open
- The library - **General Brush Strokes Library** will be in this directory
- Click onto the file to open it

- This will open up only the **Brush Palette** from the library

- Scroll down until the **Twin Needle** brush stroke is visible and click onto that brush
  *This will place the **Twin Needle** brush stroke into the **Brushes** palette of the file you are in - check the palette to see if this has happened*

Creating Binding: Delete Part Of The Top

Direct Selection Tool Hot Key **A**

- **Step 1:** Copy the front and back top
- Marquee over the left side with the **Direct Selection Tool** Hot Key **A**
- Tap the **Delete** key *once,* to delete the selection
- Do the same with the right side seam and hem, being careful not to delete any of the armhole
- Click onto the **Path**/line between the neck point and the shoulder point and tap the **Delete** key *once* only

*If you tap the **Delete** key more than **once** everything will be deleted*

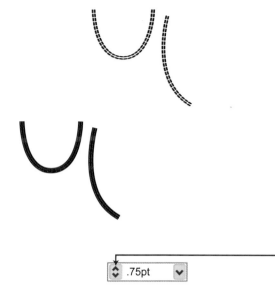

Create Binding: Stroke Sizes And Brush Strokes

Selection Tool Hot Key **V**

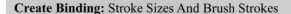

- **Step 2:** Select the armhole and neckline with the **Selection Tool** Hot Key **V** and click onto the **Two Needle Top Stitch** Brush Stroke
- Change the stroke weight to **.75** - this will be the guide to base the size of the binding
- Do not deselect
- **Step 3:** Copy the stroke Hot Key **Ctrl C** Apple OS **Cmd C** to the back Hot Key **Ctrl B** Apple OS **Cmd B**
- Change the colour of the stroke to a contrast colour () and deselect the brush stroke by clicking onto the **Remove Brush Stroke** symbol () in the **Brushes** palette
- Do *not* deselect the new lines
- Click onto the up arrow next to the stroke size and increase the stroke until it is either side of the Twin Needle stitching
- Keep these lines selected

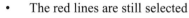

.75pt

Create Binding: Convert A Stroke Into An Outline And Adjust Binding Shapes

Direct Selection Tool Hot Key **A**
Add Anchor Point Tool Hot Key **+**

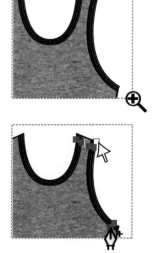

- The red lines are still selected
- **Step 4:** Go to **Object** in the menu bar
- Scroll down to **Path**
- Select **Outline Stroke**
  This will turn the stroke from a line (⬛) into a filled shape (⬛). It is now easier to manipulate the binding shape to suit the shape of the top
- Click onto black in the **Swatches** palette to put a stroke around the shape
- Change the stroke weight to **.5pt**
- Click onto the **Add Anchor Point Tool** Hot Key **+**
- **Step 5:** Add anchor points just below the points you anticipate adjusting - this will maintain the integrity of the binding shape when you adjust it
- Click onto the anchor points and adjust them so that the binding lines up with the shape of the garment
- Copy the right armhole binding to the left armhole

Reflect and Copy: See pages 43 and 44

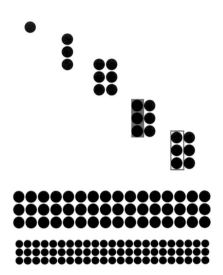

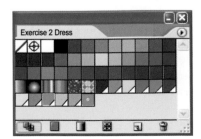

Bead Trim Around Neck Line:

Ellipse Tool Hot Key **L**

- **Step 1:** Draw a circle **2mm** circumference with the **Ellipse Tool** Hot Key **L**
- Set the keyboard increment to **2.2mm**
- **Step 2:** Copy the circle down twice, using the **Alt** key and the down direction key on the keyboard
- **Step 3:** Marquee over the three circles and copy these once more to the right to establish the repeat
- **Step 4:** Draw the repeat boundary box and **Send To The Back** Hot Key **Shift Ctrl [**
  Apple OS **Shift Cmd [**
- **Create A New Pattern Brush** (◨)
  *Remember, when you change the size of the **Stroke**, the size of the **Brush Stroke** will change*

X-Over Top - Components:

1. **Spot repeat colour change**

2. **Pencil Tool**

Spot Pattern Fill: Open A Swatch Palette Created In Another File, Change The Colour Of This Swatch

Selection Tool Hot Key **V**
Group Selection Tool No Hot Key

- **Step 1:** To retrieve a pattern swatch created in another file, follow these steps:
- Go to **Window** in the Menu Bar
  ↓
  Swatch Libraries ——┐
  ↓
  Other Library
- The file directory will open
- Follow the normal steps back to where your **"Illustrator Lessons"** folder is in your directory
- Open this folder and select the **Exercise 2 Dress** file
- This will open up only the **Swatch** palette from this file

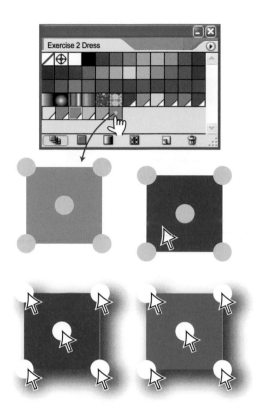

Spot Pattern Fill: Change The Colour Of This Swatch

- **Step 1:** Click onto the **Spot Pattern Swatch** and drag the swatch onto the work area
- Close the **Exercise 2 Dress** swatch palette
- The swatch is grouped
- Click onto the **Group Selection Tool** Hot Key +
- **Step 2:** Select the background colour and change the colour to red
- **Step 3:** Select the spot, holding down the **Shift** key to pick up multiple objects and change the colour to white
- **Step 4:** Select the whole pattern repeat and drag this into the **Swatches** palette
- Select the background colour again and change the colour to blue
- **Step 5:** Select and drag this into the **Swatches Palette**

Pencil Tool:

Pencil Tool Hot Key **N**

- The **Pencil Tool** lets you draw open and closed paths as if drawing with a pencil on paper. It is most useful for creating a hand-drawn look.
- **Anchor Points** are set down as you draw with the **Pencil Tool** and their position cannot be determined. However, they can be adjusted once the path is complete - use the **Pen Tool** options to do this (adding or deleting **Anchor Points**) or leave the line selected and draw over the area that needs adjusting with the **Pencil Tool**
- The number of anchor points set down is determined by the length and complexity of the line drawn. Double clicking on the **Pencil Tool** brings up a dialogue box in which the tolerances can be set. These settings control how sensitive the **Pencil Tool** is to the movement of your mouse or graphics-tablet stylus
- In this garment the **Pencil Tool** has been used to create the gathering into the knot at the back
- To change a previously drawn line: Select the line that you would like to change click onto the **Pencil Tool** Hot Key **N**
- Draw over the selected line being careful when starting to rest the point of the **Pencil Tool** on the selected line

CREATING A PATTERN WITH A SCANNED IMAGE

1. **Stripe repeat**

2. **Stripe Repeat with a scanned fabric**

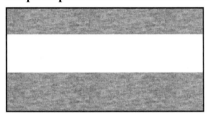

3. **Rotate stripe pattern in the garment**

Creating A Stripe Repeat:

Rectangle Tool Hot Key **M**
Selection Tool Hot Key **V**

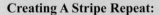

- **Step 1:** Select the **Rectangle Tool** Hot Key **M** in the Tool Box and click onto the work area to bring up the dialogue box

- Create a rectangle 20mm ✕ 30mm
- Repeat the process and create another rectangle 20mm ✕ 15mm
- **Step 2:** Select the two rectangles and place them on top of each other and align them with the **Vertical Align Bottom Tool** (▣) and the **Horizontal Align Left Tool** (▤)
- **Step 3:** Copy the back rectangle (20mm ✕ 30mm) to the back - Hot Keys **Ctrl C**; **Ctrl B** Apple OS **Cmd C**; **Cmd B**
- Do not deselect the rectangle
- Remove the colour fill

- **Step 4:** Marquee over the whole repeat and drag it into the **Swatches** palette

Creating A Stripe Repeat: Including The Scanned Plain Fabric

Rectangle Tool Hot Key **M**
Selection Tool Hot Key **V**

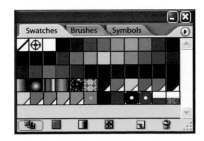

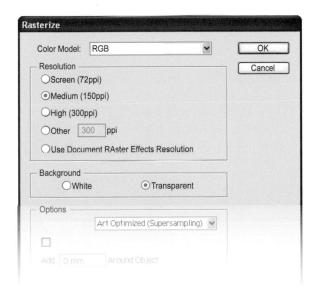

- **Step 1:** Select the **Rectangle Tool** Hot Key **M** in the **Tool Box** and click onto the work area to bring up the dialogue box
- Create a rectangle 20mm × 30mm
- Fill this with the scanned grey marle (refer to page 103)
- **Step 2:** Repeat the process and create another rectangle 20mm × 15mm
- **Step 3:** Select the two rectangles and place them on top of each other and align them with the **Vertical Align Bottom Tool** (⬛) and the **Horizontal Align Left Tool** (⬛)
- **Step 4:** The image now needs to be **Rasterized**
- Go to **Object** in the Menu Bar
  ↓
  Rasterize

- A dialogue box will appear
- The Colour Mode will be the same as the file colour mode (RGB)
- Select **Medium (150ppi)**
- **Transparent Background**
- **OK**
-
-

- **Step 5:** Create another **Rectangle** (20mm X 30mm)
- **Align** this with the rasterized image and send it to the back
  Hot Key **Shift Ctrl [** Apple OS **Shift Cmd [**
- **Step 6:** Remove the colour fill

*Rasterize - When a **Vector** image is **Rasterized** it is converted into a **Bitmap** image (refer to page 2). A pattern fill cannot be made with a pattern swatch from the **Swatches** palette because the pattern swatch has already been processed. **Rasterizing** the image simplifies it and allows the program to see the whole image as a shape not a pattern swatch*

- **Step 7:** Marquee over the whole repeat and drag it into the **Swatches** palette

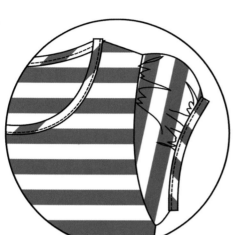

- There are two options to **Rotate** the stripe pattern fill

- **Option 1: Rotating the stripe in the binding:**

  Binding is normally cut on a 45° angle
- **Step 1:** Select the binding with the **Group Selection Tool**
- **Step 2:** Double click the **Rotate Tool** to activate the **Rotate Tool** dialogue box

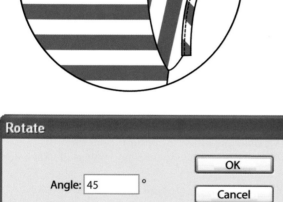

- Type **45°** into the **Angle** box;
- In the **Option** section select the **Patterns** option only
- Select **OK**
  This will rotate the stripe pattern only

- **Option 2: Rotating the stripe in the sleeve:**

  When aligning a stripe pattern fill with the hemline, it is preferable to be able to do this with a less constraining method
- **Step 1:** Select the sleeve with the **Group Selection Tool**
- The stripe fill is running horizontally
- **Step 2:** Click onto the **Rotate Tool** Hot Key **R**, hold the **Tilda (~)** key down and start to rotate the sleeve at the same time
- Rotate the shape until the line runs parallel or as close to the sleeve hem line as possible

  *The **Tilda (~)** key is located in the second row of keys on the far left above the **Tab** key, it can also be used to scale the size of a pattern*

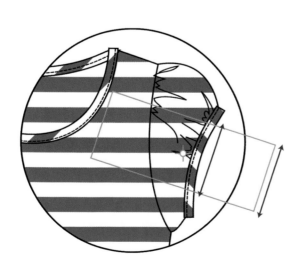

1. **Gathering brush strokes**

2. **Webbing brush stroke**

3. **Embroidery brush stroke**

Retrieving The Gathering Pattern Brushes:

- Open the **General Brush Strokes** library (refer to page 106)

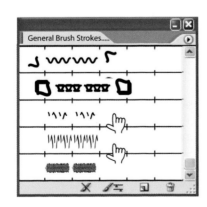

- Scroll down until the **Gathering** brush strokes are visible and click onto the brushes
  This will place the brush strokes into the Brushes palette of the file you are in - check the palette to see if this has happened

Creating A Webbing Pattern Brush:

Selection Tool Hot Key **V**
Direct Selection Tool Hot Key **A**
Rectangle Tool Hot Key **M**
Rotate Tool Hot Key **R**

- **Step 1:** Draw a rectangle 8mm × 8mm
- Rotate the rectangle 45° using the **Shift** key
- Set the **Weight** of the stroke to **3pt**
- Delete the left corner of the rotated square to leave an arrow facing right
- Set the keyboard increment to 2mm and copy the line five times

- **Step 2:** Select all six lines and **Outline** them
- Go to **Object** in the menu bar
- Scroll down to **Path**
- Select **Outline Stroke**

- **Step 3:** Select the **Outline View**
  Hot Key **Ctrl Y** Apple OS **Cmd Y**
- Click onto the **Rectangle Tool** Hot Key **M** and find the repeat as per the illustration below
- Go back to the **Preview View**

- **Step 4:** Send the repeat rectangle to the back
  Hot Key **Shift Ctrl [** Apple OS **Shift Cmd [**
- Set the keyboard increment to 20mm
- Copy the repeat rectangle to the right using the **Direction Arrows** and the **Keyboard Increment**
  *The reason being the rectangle can be replaced in the exact same position once you are ready to create the **Pattern Brush***

Creating A Webbing Pattern Brush:

- **Step 5:** Select the whole image and click onto the **Divide** icon () in the **Pathfinder** palette
- Delete everything except the repeat

- **Step 6:** Move the repeat boundary box back behind the image
- Remove the colour from the boundary rectangle
- Marquee over the whole image and create a **New Brush Stroke**

- Create a **New Brush Stroke**
- Click onto the **New Brush** icon ()
- Select **New Pattern Brush**
- Click onto **OK**
- Follow the **New Brush Stroke** option instructions on page 54

- The brush has a transparent background and the colour in the brush can be changed.

- **Step 7:** Place the brush stroke into the skirt:

- Following the drape of the skirt draw a line
- Increase the stroke weight to 3.5 pt

- Copy the stroke on top of the stroke just created
  Hot Key **Ctrl C** Apple OS **Cmd C**
  Hot Key **Ctrl F** Apple OS **Cmd F**
- Change the colour of the stroke to a deeper colour and select the **Webbing Brush** - the stroke weight will default to **1 pt**
- Adjust the stroke weight until the brush fits within the solid stroke

Creating An Embroidery Pattern Brush:

Selection Tool Hot Key **V**
Direct Selection Tool Hot Key **A**
Rectangle Tool Hot Key **M**
Pen Point Tool Hot Key **P**
Rotate Tool Hot Key **R**

- **Step 1:** Use the **Webbing Brush** as a guide for the size of the embroidery brush
- Draw a vertical line using the **Shift** key
- Rotate/copy the line from the bottom anchor point (refer to page 13 - note dragging the rotate axis point)
- Adjust the length of the lines with the **Direct Selection Tool** Hot Key **A**

- **Step 2:** Select the lines on the left of the centre line and reflect and copy them

- **Step 3:** Create the arrow at the top of the image by drawing the vertical line and then the angled lines

- **Step 4:** Copy the arrow by selecting it and pressing the **Alt** key at the same time as dragging it into position
- Once the arrow is in position rotate it 45° by clicking onto the **Rotate Tool** Hot Key **R** and start to rotate before pressing **Shift** to rotate it **45°**

Creating An Embroidery Pattern Brush:

- **Step 5:** Draw the pattern repeat boundary box over the brush stroke and send it to the back
  Hot Key **Ctrl Shift [** Apple OS **Cmd Shift [**

- Remove the colour and marquee over the whole image
- Create a **New Brush Stroke**
- Click onto the **New Brush** icon (⬛)
- Select **New Pattern Brush**
- Click onto **OK**
- A dialogue box will pop up with the brush in the first tile
- Name the new stitch - **Embroidery Brush**
- Leave the **Scale** at **100%** and the **Spacing** at **0%**
- Click onto **Stretch to fit** (⊙)
- Click onto the arrow to bring up the *"Colorization"* **Method** options
- Select **Hue Shift**
- **OK**

Placing the embroidery brush stroke on top of the webbing brush stroke:

- **Step 1:** Copy the **Webbing Brush** stroke in front again Hot Key **Ctrl C** Apple OS **Cmd C**
  Hot Key **Ctrl F** Apple OS **Cmd F**
- **Step 2:** Change the colour of the stroke back to the lighter blue and select the **Embroidery Brush** - the stroke weight will default to 1pt
- **Step 3:** Copy the **Embroidery Brush** stroke in front again Hot Key **Ctrl C** Apple OS **Cmd C**
  Hot Key **Ctrl F** Apple OS **Cmd F**
- **Step 4:** Remove the brush stroke by clicking onto the **Remove Brush Stroke** symbol (❌) in the **Brushes** palette
- **Step 5:** Move this line down using the direction arrows on the keyboard and change the line to a dashed line

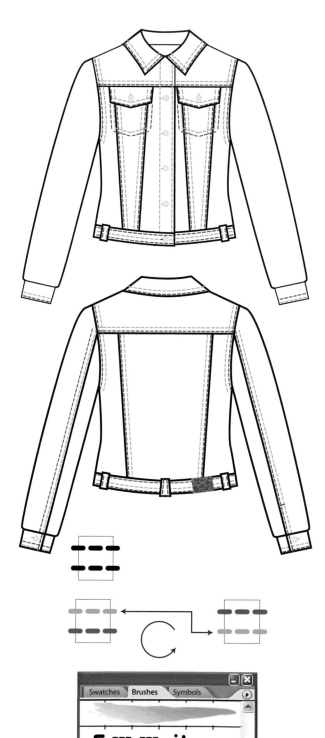

Jacket - Components:

1. **Two colour brush stroke**

2. **Stud Button - changing gradient colours**

3. **Printed and embroidered leather badge**

Creating A Two Colour Pattern Brush:

Direct Selection Tool Hot Key **A**

- **Step 1:** Create the two colour Twin Needle brush stroke (refer to the top of page 54)
- **Step 2:** Change the stitch colours to the two blues
- Select the whole image and create a new **Pattern Brush**
- **Step 4:** Name the new stitch - **2 Colour Twin Wide Needle**
- Leave the **Scale** at **100%** and the **Spacing** at **0%**
- Click onto **Stretch to fit (⊙)**
- Do not click onto the arrow to bring up the *"Colorization"* **Method** options
- Leave this on the default option **None**
  The brush stroke is already the colour you need
- **OK**
- **Step 5:** Rotate the image 180º as it is a one way brush stroke and create a new **Pattern Brush**

GRADIENT COLOUR CHANGE

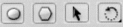

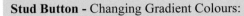

Stud Button - Changing Gradient Colours:

Ellipse Tool Hot Key **L**
Polygon Tool No Hot Key
Selection Tool Hot Key **V**
Rotate Tool Hot Key **R**

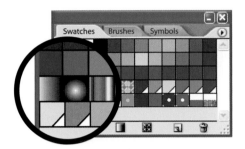

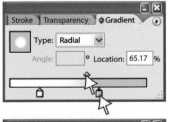

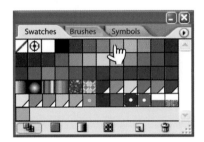

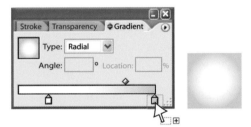

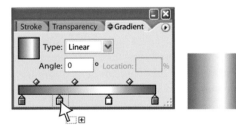

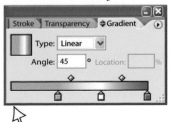

- The stud button is made up of a circle with a **Radial Gradient** and two **Polygons** on top of each other and filled with a **Linear Gradient**
- **Step 1:** Draw an **Ellipse** Hot Key **L** 22mm in circumference
- **Step 2:** Fill the **Ellipse** with a **Radial Gradient** from the default **Swatches** palette
- **Step 3:** Draw the **Polygon** and fill it with the **Linear** Gradient Swatch from the **Swatches** palette
- **Step 4:** Copy the polygon to the front, scale it down and rotate it to give the polygon the appearance of a jewel

- Change the colour of the gradient by selecting the colour you want from the **Swatches** palette and drag it into the colour swatch on the gradient colour bar

- You can drag as many colours as you wish onto the colour bar

- The distribution of colour in the gradient can be varied by moving the colour blocks under the colour bar to the left or right
- The intensity of the division between the colours can be varied by moving the diamond on top of the colour bar and the colour blocks closer together or further apart

- The angle of the linear gradient can be changed by typing the degree of the angle into the **Gradient** option box
- Colours can also be removed by placing the cursor onto that colour and dragging it off the colour bar

Printed And Embroidered Leather Badge: Masking Objects And Turning A Font Into Outlines

Rectangle Tool Hot Key M
Pen Tool Hot Key **P**
Selection Tool Hot Key **V**
Type Tool Hot Key **T**

- **Step 1:** Draw a rectangle 60mm × 40mm
- **Step 2:** Create the design to go onto the badge with the **Pen Tool** Hot Key **P**
- Type the logo and choose the font from the font list

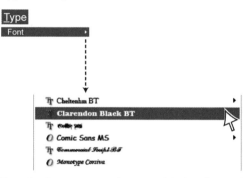

- **Step 3:** Once you are happy with the size and position of the word it should be turned into an **Outline**
- Go to **Type** in the Menu Bar

  Create Outlines

*Changing the word from a **Font** into an **Outline** allows the word to be read as a vector image and not a font (fonts are unique to the computer you are working on and may not be available on another computer). This needs to be done when supplying a soft copy of finished art to manufacturers.*

- **Step 4:** Select the rectangle and bring it to the front Hot Key **Shift Ctrl]** Apple OS **Shift Cmd]**
- Marquee over the whole image to select it and mask the images with the top image (refer to page 94)
- Go to **Object** in the Menu Bar

  Clipping Mask

  Make
  Hot Key **Ctrl 7** Apple OS **Cmd 7**

- **Step 5:** Draw a rectangle within the shape of the badge to depict the stitching

Shorts - Components:

1. **Denim Scan**

2. **Wash Treatment - Transparency** palette

Scan The Denim:

- Scan in an actual piece of denim, both the face side and the reverse sides and save each separately as a JPEG or TIFF file onto your **C Drive**
  ↓
  Adobe Illustrator Exercises
  ↓
  Denim Scan Face
  ↓
  and **Denim Scan Reverse**

- Please note all scanners are different and there are two points to consider:
  1) Scan the image at 200 DPI (dots per inch)
  2) Scan this image in colour
  For all other instructions follow the scanner instructions

- If your scanner allows, crop the image to about 10cm × 10cm before scanning

Wash Treatment - Transparency Palette:

Group Selection Tool No Hot Key
Eye Dropper Tool Hot Key **I**
Mesh Tool Hot Key **U**

- **Step 1:** Select each front leg of the shorts with the **Group Selection Tool** and copy this to the front
  Hot Key **Ctrl C** Apple OS **Cmd C**
  Hot Key **Ctrl F** Apple OS **Cmd F**
- **Step 2:** Fill this shape with a plain colour that is close to the denim scan colour - you can **Eye Drop** Hot Key **I** the denim scan to find a close match
  *The denim that you **Eye Drop** must be the original scan not a **Pattern Fill** - as the pattern fill is now read as a colour when you place the Eye Dropper on it*
- Deselect the front shorts
- **Step 2:** Click onto the **Mesh Tool** Hot Key **U**
- Change the colour in the fill box to white ( )
  The colour in the stroke box is of no consequence with this tool
- Click onto the plain front shorts (see the left leg in the illustration) to add what will become the sanded or washed treatment
- See the right leg in the illustration
  *Note - using the **Mesh Tool** in this way works best with a simple shape (in Chapter 5 we will demonstrate what to do with more complex shapes)*

Transparency Palette

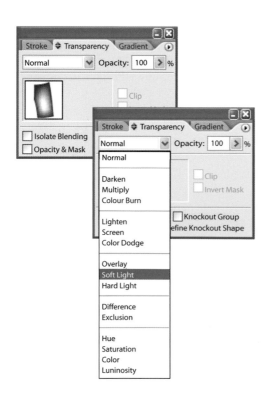

- The **Transparency** palette has a number of options. We would strongly encourage you to experiment with this palette as the results vary with the colours and finish you would like to depict
- The **Transparency** palette would have opened up as a linked palette with the **Stroke** and **Gradient** palettes
- When you open the **Transparency** palette the selected shape will appear as a thumbnail
- The default **Transparency** setting is normal
- Click onto the down arrow to reveal the **Transparency** options
- Select **Soft Light** to achieve the same finish as the illustration on page 117

Dress - Components:

1. **Broderie Anglaise pattern fill**

2. **Broderie Anglaise pattern brush**

3. **Broderie Anglaise scalloped edge pattern brush**

Broderie Anglaise Pattern Fill:

Rectangle Tool Hot Key **M**
Ellipse Tool Hot Key **L**
Pen Tool Hot Key **P**
Direct Selection Tool Hot Key **A**

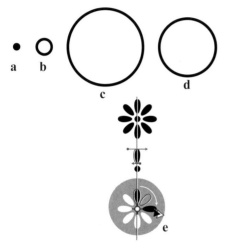

- **Step 1:** Create the repeat boundary box for the Broderie Anglaise pattern repeat
- Click onto the **Rectangle Tool** Hot Key **M** and create a rectangle with a width of 30mm and a length of 125mm
- Lock the boundary rectangle by clicking onto **Object** in the menu bar
  ↓
  Lock
  ↓
  Lock Selection Hot Key **Ctrl 2** Apple OS **Cmd 2**

- **Step 2:** Draw the components for the design
  a: An **Ellipse** 1mm × 1mm with fill only
  b: An **Ellipse** 2mm × 2 mm with a 1pt stroke only
  c: An **Ellipse** 10mm × 10mm
  d: An **Ellipse** 7.5mm × 7.5mm
  e: A flower that will fit within a 7.5mm circle (refer to page 13 for rotate and copy)

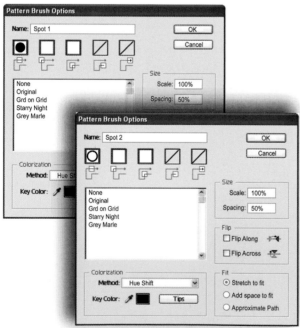

- **Step 3:** Create brush strokes out of the two smaller circles
  Note the difference with these two brush strokes
- Select the first circle and click onto the **New Brush** icon (⬛)
- Select **New Pattern Brush**
- Click onto **OK**
- A dialogue box will pop up with the brush in the first tile
- Name the new stitch - **Spot 1**
- Leave the **Scale** at **100%**
- Change **Spacing** to **50%**
- Click onto **Stretch to fit** (⊙)
- Click onto the arrow to bring up the *"Colorization"* **Method** options
- Select **Hue Shift** and **OK**
- Repeat this for the second circle - **Spot 2** brush

- **Step 4:** Place the 7.5mm and 10mm circles within each other and the flower within that - **Vertical Align Centre** (▣) and **Horizontal Align Centre** (▣)
- Delete the top anchor points of the circles with the **Direct Selection Tool** Hot Key **A**

- **Step 5:** Select the inside line and put the **Spot 1** brush stroke into it, changing the **Stroke** to .75pt
- Select the outside line and create a zig-zag (refer to page 85) **Size: .15** and **Ridges: 55**
- Select **Corner**
- Change the **Stroke** to **.5**

- **Step 6:** Create the four dot eyelet motif as in the illustration, group the motif and place it above the flower
- Align the whole motif with the **Horizontal Align Centre** (⊞) option in the **Align** palette
- Copy the eyelet motif to the top of the right zig-zag scallop and **Group** the whole image

- **Step 7:** Place the motif you have just created at the left edge of the repeat rectangle
- Change the keyboard increment to 10mm
- Copy the motif twice using the direction keys and the **Alt** key
- **Ungroup** the motif and copy the lower eyelet motif to the opposite edge of the boundary rectangle
- Place a flower on the edge of the repeat and copy it over to the opposite edge - you can still have the keyboard increment at 10mm, just tap the direction key twice
- **Group** the whole image again

- **Step 8:** Draw a circle 30mm × 30mm
- Change the line to the **Spot 1** brush stroke
- Draw another circle 25mm × 25mm and place that within the bigger circle
- Change that line to the **Spot 2** brush stroke
- Align both circles - **Vertical Align Centre** (⊞) and **Horizontal Align Centre** (⊞)
- Delete the top **Anchor Point** of both circles
- Group the two half circles and place them above the first line of motifs
- Select the whole image and **Horizontal Align Centre** (⊞)
- Select the lower circle and **Expand** it
- Go to **Object** in the menu bar
  ↳**Expand Appearance**
Expand Appearance will turn the brush stroke back into vector objects - each object or spot can be manipulated
- Select the last two spots, as highlighted in the illustration and delete them

Broderie Anglaise Pattern Fill Continued:

- **Step 9:** Follow the illustration, placing the two flowers in the centre of the repeat, scaling them to suit the size of the repeat
- The top flower is a **Stroke** only and the bottom flower is a **Fill** only
- Place the eyelet motif on either side of these flowers and **Vertical Align Centre** (⊞)
- Group the two eyelet motifs
- Select the whole image and **Horizontal Align Centre** (⊞)
- Create another 25mm × 25mm circle and place this above the last flower
- Change the line to the **Spot 2** brush stroke
- Count out four spots either side of the centre spot and cut the circle, delete the bottom part of the circle

- **Step 10:** Follow the illustration and create two rows of eyelets and flowers
- Make the repeat as the illustration - three flowers in the bottom row and four flowers in the top row
  Note: always copy what happens on the edge of the repeat from one side to the other
- Group the two rows of flowers and eyelets

- **Step 11:** Select the grouped image and move it up holding the **Shift** and **Alt** key down at the same time
  This will move the image in a vertical line and copy it maintaining the correct alignment of the image
- The last performed action can be repeated by going to **Object** in the menu bar
  ↳**Transform** ⟶ **Transform Again**
    Hot Key **Ctrl D** Apple OS **Cmd D**
- Repeat this process until the total vertical repeat is filled

Broderie Anglaise Pattern Fill Continued:

- **Step 12:** Set the **Keyboard Increment** to **125 mm** and copy the top row of flowers and eyelets down to the border of the design
- Likewise copy the scalloped border to the top

- **Step 13:** Change the colour to the colours of the Broderie Anglaise - in the illustration the colours depict tonal white Broderie Anglaise (refer to page 59 - select same colour)

- **Step 14:** Unlock the boundary rectangle by clicking onto **Object** in the menu bar
  ↓
  Unlock All
  Hot Key **Shift Ctrl 2** Apple OS **Shift Cmd 2**
- The boundary rectangle will be selected
- Copy this to the back
  Hot Key **Ctrl C** Apple OS **Cmd C**
  Hot Key **Ctrl B** Apple OS **Cmd B**
- Remove the fill from this rectangle to create the boundary box for the repeat
- Select the whole image and drag it into the swatch box

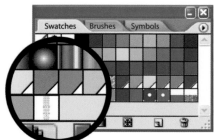

- The pattern is now ready to be used as a pattern fill
- You can name the file by double clicking on the swatch and a dialogue box will come up with an option to name the swatch

Broderie Anglaise Brush Stroke:

- **Step 1:** This brush stroke will be used in the skirt and will follow the curve of the hem
- Use the same image with the following changes:
  a: Delete the row of eyelets and flowers at the bottom of the image
  b: Delete the scallops at the top of the image
  c: Delete the filled rectangle and leave the transparent boundary rectangle

Broderie Anglaise Brush Stroke Continued:

- **Step 2:** Select the whole image and click onto the **New Brush** icon (⬛)
- Select **New Pattern Brush**
- Click onto **OK**
- A dialogue box will pop up with the brush in the first tile
- Name the new stitch - **Broderie Anglaise**
- Leave the **Scale** at **100%** and the
- Leave the **Spacing** at **0%**
- Click onto **Stretch to fit** (◉)
- Leave the *"Colorization"* **Method** on the default **None** option
- **OK**

Broderie Anglaise Brush Stroke Placed In The Skirt:

- **Step 1:** Draw a gently curved line that follows the curve of the hem
- Place this line behind the skirt shape
- **Step 2:** Mask the line using the skirt shape as the **Clipping Mask** Hot Key **Ctrl 7** Apple OS **Cmd 7**

This brush stroke is a very deep brush stroke and because of this it will distort if the line drawn has detailed curves

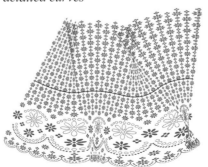

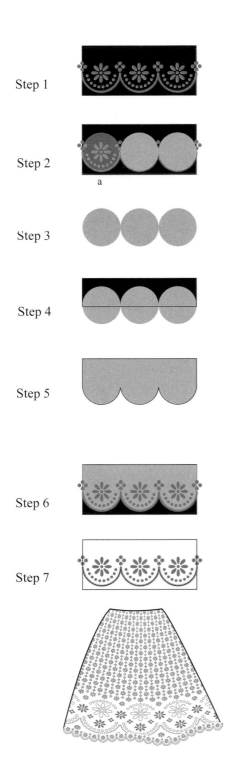

Step 1

Step 2

a

Step 3

Step 4

Step 5

Step 6

Step 7

Scalloped Broderie Anglaise Edging Brush Stroke:

Selection Tool Hot Key **V**
Ellipse Tool Hot Key **L**

- **Step 1:** The same image will be used to create this brush stroke with the following changes
  a: Delete everything but the scallop repeat and the boundary rectangle
  b: Scale the length of the rectangle to just above the scallops and put a fill into the rectangle
- **Step 2:** The design will now need a fill in the shape of the scallops across the repeat
- Draw an **Ellipse** 10mm × 10mm
- Align the circle with the first scallop design on the left side of the whole design **a**
- Change the Keyboard increment back to 10mm
- Copy the circle across to the right twice more
- **Step 3: Group** and move these circles down or aside using the direction keys/ keyboard increment

- **Step 4:** Copy the rectangle and move it to be positioned behind the three circles
- Adjust the vertical length of the rectangle until the bottom half of the circles are revealed
- **Horizontal Align Left (▤)**

- **Step 5:** Select the circles and the rectangle and ungroup the circles, do not deselect
- Click onto the **Add To Shape Area Tool** (▣) in the **Pathfinder** palette, **Expand** to create one shape
- **Step 6:** Place the solid scallops behind the Broderie image in line with the boundary rectangle
- Check that the boundary rectangle is at the back of the image - to do this, place a colour fill into the rectangle
- **Step 7:** Check the position and remove the colour
- Select the whole image and drag it into the **Brushes** palette

- Create a new pattern brush - **Broderie Scallop**

Creating The Flower In The Background:

 or

Pen Tool Hot Key **P**
Pencil Tool Hot Key **N**
Selection Tool Hot Key **V**

The flower in the background of the story board has been extracted from a digital photograph, it has been masked and the colour changed to suit the colours of the story board

- **Step 1:** Open up the digital photograph in Adobe Illustrator

- **Step 2:** Zoom up to the area you wish to extract
- Click onto the **Pen Tool** Hot Key **P** and draw around the section of the photograph to be masked
  *The **Pencil Tool** Hot Key N can also be used - however it is easier to use the pencil tool if you are using a stylus not a mouse (refer to page 107)*

- **Step 3:** Copy the shape away from the photograph
  Hot Keys **Ctrl C, Ctrl V**
  Apple OS **Cmd C, Cmd V**

- **Step 4:** Select the photograph and the vector flower shape and **Make A Clipping Mask**
  Hot Key **Ctrl 7** Apple OS **Cmd 7** (refer to page 116)

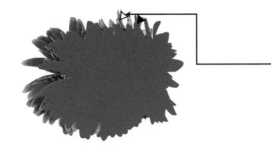

Creating The Flower In The Background Continued:

- **Step 5:** Click onto the copied flower shape and put a blue fill into it (▣)
- Place the filled shape exactly on top of the masked shape - *remember when you place one anchor point directly on top of another, the selection arrow goes white*
- Send the blue flower shape to the back
  Hot Key **Shift Ctrl [** Apple OS **Shift Cmd [**
- Deselect the blue flower

- **Step 6:** Select the masked photograph and go to the **Transparency** palette (refer to page 118)
- Click onto the down arrow to reveal the transparency options

- Select **Luminosity**
  Luminosity creates a result colour with the hue and saturation of the solid colour flower shape and the luminance or light of the photograph. This effect works best with a bitmap image and there are soft graduations of colour

- The flowers can now be copied and manipulated - on this story board they have been made **Transparent** and have been **Rotated** and **Scaled**

Type And Type Along A Path:

- Place the flowers onto the story board
- Type titles next to each style
- Create a curved path around the flowers and type the story board theme onto it (refer to pages 26 and 27 for Type instructions)

Chapter 4 is complete. The finished story board is illustrated on page 128

White washed
denim jacket

1 x 1 rib top
with bead trim

Elastic waist
voile skirt

Drop waist
x-over top

Broderie dress

Denim shorts

Yarn-dyed stripe top

Girls 8-14

Spring into summer in the freshest of blus

BLU-D

CHAPTER 5

STORY BOARDS

Fashion Sketches

Chapter 5 introduces Adobe Photoshop. It should be noted that Adobe Photoshop is only a means to an end. We use it as a minor tool to manipulate images that cannot be manipulated in Adobe Illustrator.

Croquis - *(Pronounced - kro-ke)*

A French word meaning a rough sketch. Fashion Designers have adapted this word to refer to the figurative templates used to speed up the process of illustrating their designs.

The method used for developing a male or female croquis is very similar with some variations:

Female:
Slender
Leggy

Male:
Smaller head and squarer jaw
Thicker neck and broader shoulders
Torso tapered to narrower hips
Well defined muscles in arms and legs
Thicker hands and feet

When taking a photograph of either a male or female you can give the allusion of height by positioning yourself lower than the model. When choosing a photograph, the pose should emphasise the most important features. The aim is to capture the fashion look but not to obscure the garment design. The photograph chosen has the figure in a relaxed pose, the majority of his weight is on his left leg.

Equipment needed:
- Photograph of a figure
- Drawing board or table
- Tape
- Ruler or L square
- 2 Sheets of tracing paper longer than the photograph
- HB pencil
- Black felt-tip pen
- Eraser
- Scanner, computer and printer

Hand Trace Croquis:

- **Step 1:** Select your photograph carefully keeping in mind the garments you want to illustrate on it.

- Tape the photograph to the drawing board

- Rule a line through the **Pit of the Neck** and at right angles to the floor. This is the **Balance Line**

  The tracing paper must be longer than the photograph

- Draw an identical line onto the tracing paper

Hand Trace The Figure And Elongate:

- **Step 2:** Place the tracing paper over the top of the photograph and **line up the axis** on both sheets

- Starting at the top, draw in the head making it smaller with a square jaw

- Move the tracing paper up a fraction and draw in the neck and broaden the shoulders

- Draw in the outline of the torso, arms and hands with well defined muscles in the arms

- **Step 3:** Draw in the legs to the knees

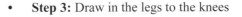

- Mark in the new position of the feet as indicated by the horizontal line. In this instance it is a head difference

- **Step 4:** Move the tracing paper up to match the position of the feet on the photograph.
- **Make certain that the axes match**

- Draw in the legs with well defined muscles

The extent to which you elongate the figure depends on the client you are working for and your style of drawing. e.g. street wear or corporate uniforms. This technique is not based on the 7½ heads to 8½ heads.

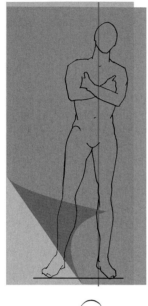

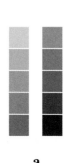

a

b

- **Step 5:** Remove the photograph and place a second sheet of tracing paper over the drawing

- Draw over the figure with a black felt tipped pen, making certain that **all lines are joined/closed**

  This is essential for the next process of scanning the figure into the computer

Computer Trace and Shading:

Rectangle Tool Hot Key **M**
Pen Tool Hot Key **P**

Scanning - each scanner is different
(refer to page 31, Steps 3 and 4)

- **Step 6:** Once the scanned image has been converted into a vector image following the instructions on pages 32-33 Steps 5-7, save and print the file

- If shading is to be added to the figure you can plan this by rendering the printout
  Note: keep in mind the light source

- **Step 7:** Before commencing to render the figure, test the colours to be used. What appears on the computer screen may be entirely different to the hard copy from the printer. Each printer and different types of paper will produce different results. It is therefore advisable to test print the colours on the paper and printer to be used in the final product

  a. Colour used from the **Adobe Illustrator Swatch Libraries - Skintones**

  b. Colour the figure in the selected colour

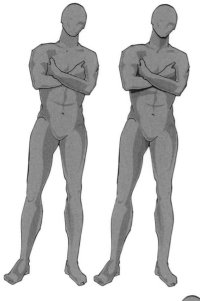

Shading:

Pen Tool Hot Key **P**

- **Step 8:** Use the hand rendering as a guide. Draw in the basic shaded shapes - lightest tones first, using the **Pen Tool** Hot Key **P**

- Fill with colour and using the **Transparency** palette set the **Opacity** to **50%**

- Repeat this process using a degree of darker flesh tone - transparency should stay at 50%

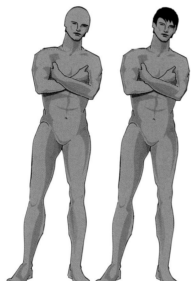

Facial Features And Hair:

Pen Tool Hot Key **P**

- **Step 9:** Draw in the facial features

- Draw in the hair

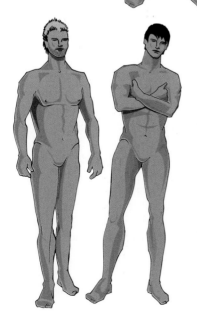

Once this technique is mastered it is advisable to create a library of varying poses and styles of croquis to speed up the process of producing finished art work.

- Save this file and name it **Male Croquis Library**

Creating Story Board 1:

Story Board 1 is made up of four layers

- **Layer 1:** Consists of the background photo taken with a digital camera and opened up in Illustrator. The colour is changed to Grey Tones and the **Film Grain** effect is applied
- **Layer 2:** The garments are drawn onto one of the croquis created in the previous exercise
- **Layer 3:** Is made up of technical drawings of Tee shirts, colour applied and distorted with the Scribble Tool. A description of each garment is also added
- **Layer 4:** Colour swatches and text are drawn up considering the layout of the composition

The JPEG (Joint Photographic Experts Group) is a compression format and is most commonly used in digital cameras. Once loaded onto your computer you should save the image to a **TIFF** or **AI** file. If you close an image, then reopen it and save it again as JPEG format, you apply a further compression. Save to JPEG format only after you finish the composition.

Digital Photograph: Edit To Grayscale

- **Step 1:** File Open
- The image can be much larger than the A4 printable page
- Plan the final composition, considering all elements including fabric swatches, technical drawings and mood photographs, which may be included in the presentation. These can be done as rough sketches by hand. As a general rule do not place another image, for example fabric, over the focal point - in this instance it is the male.
- At this stage consider whether your final presentation should be **Landscape** or **Portrait**
- If the page is to be bound allowances must be made for a wider margin - top or left hand side

- **Step 2:** Scale the image to fit the page considering the planned layout
- Holding the **Shift** key will scale the image proportionately, do not be tempted to drag or distort a background image with a person in it

Rasterize and Grayscale:

- **Step 3:** Click onto **Object** in the menu bar

  Rasterize
- Select **Color Model: Grayscale**
- **High** (300dpi)
- **OK**

  By rasterizing the image first, your file will be smaller than if you went straight into the next step

- To adjust the tone click onto **Filter** in the menu bar

  Colors → Adjust Color
- An option box will appear
- Color Mode: **Grayscale**
- Select the **Preview** option (☑) and the **Convert** option (☑)

  Adjust the tone by using the slide bar

Film Grain:

- **Step 4:** Go to **Effects** in the menu bar

  Artistic

  Film Grain
- Different effects can be achieved by experimenting with the values in the **Effects** palette
- The illustrated effect was achieved with the following values: **Grain 4, Highlight Area 0, Intensity 10**, or you may wish to experiment with the other effects: for example - **Poster Edges**

Creating A Mask:

- **Step 5:** Create a rectangle the size of the area to be masked
- Take note of the composition

- **Step 6:** Marquee over the image and the rectangle
- Right click the mouse, a pop-up menu will appear, select **Make Clipping Mask** Hot Key **Ctrl 7** Apple OS **Cmd 7**

!REMEMBER!
*Save the file Hotkey **Ctrl S** Apple OS **Cmd S***

Male Croquis: Trousers and Tee shirt

Pen Tool Hot Key **P**
Add Anchor Points Tool Hot Key **+**
Direct Selection Tool Hot Key **A**

- **Step 1:** Create a new layer (Layer 2) following directions outlined on pages 33 and 34
- Lock **Layer 1** in the **Layers** palette
- From the croquis developed, select one appropriate to the garments you are illustrating and the composition of your story board. Open the file, copy it and paste it into the story board file
- It is preferable to lock down the figure at this stage: **Object → Lock Selection** Hot Key **Ctrl 2** Apple OS **Cmd 2**
- Draw in the shoes then the trousers. Always create shapes from the back to the front

- **Step 2:** Draw in the Tee shirt over the top of the trousers and around the arms. Repeat this process for the top section of the Tee shirt. Fill both shapes with white and a black stroke (outline). Anchor points can be added to give the effects of folds by using the **Add Anchor Point Tool** Hot Key **+** or use the Pencil Tool Hot Key **N** (refer to page 107)
- This garment shape will be used as the highlight

- **Step 3:** Duplicate both sections of the garment and reduce width wise
- Fill these shapes with the desired colour and remove the outline. Place back onto the figure and if necessary adjust the shape using the **Direct Selection Tool** Hot Key **A**. The white highlight should be on the opposite side to the shadow. Draw in the details such as seams and top stitching

- **Step 4:** Click onto **Object → Unlock All** Hot Key **Alt Ctrl 2** Apple OS **Alt Cmd 2** to release the croquis
- Marquee over the whole figure, right click and a pop-up menu will appear, select **Group** Hot Key **Ctrl G** Apple OS **Cmd G**

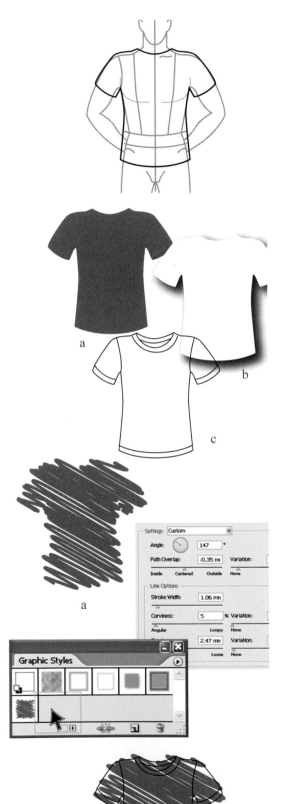

- **Step 1:** Create a new layer (Layer 3) following directions outlined on pages 33 and 34
- Lock **Layer 2** in the **Layers** palette
- Select the **Pen Tool** Hot Key **P** and draw a tee shirt shape, using the Male Croquis as a guide (refer to pages 42 - 45)

- **Step 2**
  a: Take the tee shirt off the croquis, fill with colour and remove the outline
  b: Duplicate this tee shirt, fill with white and leave the outline off
  c: Duplicate again and remove the fill colour and add a black outline
  Divide off the sleeves (refer to pages 34-38)
  Add all necessary details as line drawings only with no fill. Marquee and group

- **Step 3**
  a: Scribble effect - to give the appearance of marker strokes, click onto the coloured tee shirt and go to **Effects**

     ↓
    Stylise ⟶ **Scribble**

  The **Scribble Option** dialogue box will allow you to change the **Angle**, **Stroke Width**, **Curviness** and **Spacing**
  Once the desired effect has been achieved, save the settings in the **Graphic Styles** palette
  This can be accessed through **Window** ⟶ **Graphic Styles** Hot Key **Shift F5**
  Drag and drop the shape into this palette and click onto the **Break Link To Symbol** icon (⟜⟜). To save this library for use in other files, go to the **Graphic Styles** palette and click onto the outward arrow at the top right hand corner. Click onto **Save Graphic Style Library** and name the file. To open this effect in the future: go to **Window**

     ↓
    Graphic Style Libraries
- Click onto the required file

- **Step 4:** Move each shape on top of each other
  a: coloured scribble
  b: white without outline
  c: black outline without fill
  Marquee over all shapes and group Hot Key **Ctrl G**
  Apple OS **Cmd G**

a

b

c

d

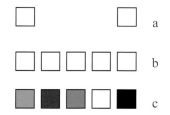

e

f

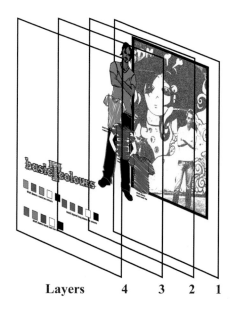

Layers   4   3   2   1

a

b

c

Text Stylised with Scribble Effect:

Type Tool Hot Key **T**
Selection Tool Hot Key **V**
Blend Tool Hot Key **W**
Rotation Tool Hot Key **R**

- **Step 1:** Create a new Layer (**Layer 4**) following directions outlined on pages 33 and 34
- Lock **Layer 3** in the **Layers** palette

Step 2: Text

a: Select the **Type Tool** Hot Kcy **T** and change the font style if required (the font used here is PROMPT Regular)
b: To change the font size highlight the desired text, right click the mouse and select the font size. The same applies if you want to change the font style
c: Change from fill to outline only
d: Click onto the **Selection Tool** Hot Key **V** and highlight the text. Click onto **Type** in the menu bar **Create Outline** Hot Key **Shift Ctrl O** Apple OS **Shift Cmd O**
Right click and ungroup
With the **Selection Tool** Hot Key **V** marquee over the text that you want to reposition, and move into place. Marquee over all and group
e: Follow instructions on page 138 Steps 2, 3 and 4
f: Rotate the image using the **Rotation Tool** Hot Key **R**

Step 3: Colour Swatches

a: Click onto the **Rectangle Tool** Hot Key **M** (white fill) and create the first colour swatch Duplicate it for the last swatch
b: Click onto the **Blend Tool** Hot Key **W**. Click onto the first swatch then click onto the last swatch. Double click onto the **Blend Tool**, an option box will appear, **Spacing, Specified Steps → 3 → OK**
c: Selection Tool Hot Key **V** click onto the swatches **Object → Expand**, right click with the mouse, **Ungroup** Hot Key **Shift Ctrl G** Apple OS **Shift Cmd G**, click away. Fill each swatch with colour. Marquee over all swatches and regroup

The composition is now complete

cotton jersey, mock double poloshirt with coverstitch hems & front placement print

cotton jersey tee-shirt with front impact placement print

cotton jersey tee-shirt with front placement print

Creating Story Board 2:
Tee Shirt Stylised With The Pencil Tool

Pen Tool Hot Key **P**
Pencil Tool Hot Key **N**

Story board 2 consists of tee shirts using the Male Youth Symbol Library and stylised using the pencil tool. Each tee shirt has a different placement print, using the same elements to make up the whole print

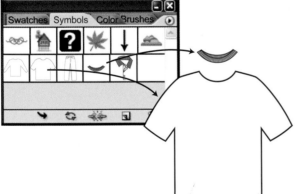

- **Step 1:** Open the Male Youth Symbol Library and select the short sleeve tee shirt and the rib neckband
- Click onto the **Break Link To Symbol** icon ( )

- **Step 2:** Double click onto the **Pencil Tool** to reveal the options
- **Fidelity** controls how far the mouse or stylus moves before a new anchor point is added to the path
- The fidelity for this tee shirt is 2.5. This means that every 2.5 pixels an anchor point is added to the path
- The higher the fidelity, the smoother the line
- **Smoothness** controls the amount of smoothing that is applied when you use the tool
- **Keep Selected** determines whether or not the path remains selected after it is drawn
- **Edit Selected Paths** determines whether or not you can change an existing path with the **Pencil Tool** within a certain tolerance. This means how close the cursor has to be before the selected line will be altered
- For the purpose of this exercise this option must be selected

Pencil Tool Preferences

Tolerances

Fidelity: 2.5 pixels

Smoothness: 10 %

OK

Cancel

Reset

Options

☐ Fill new pencil strokes

☑ Keep selected

☑ Edit selected paths

Fidelity: 12 pixels

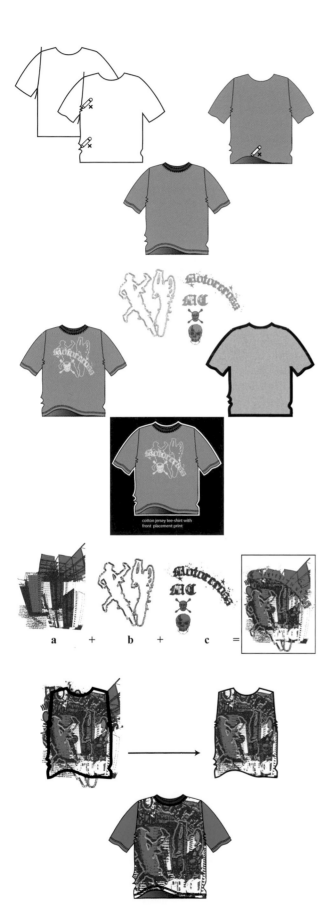

cotton jersey tee-shirt with
front placement print

a + b + c =

Tee Shirt Stylised With The Pencil Tool Continued:

- **Step 3:** Draw the sleeve design lines and alter them with the **Pencil Tool** Hot Key **N** and divide
- **Step 4:** Select the body of the tee shirt and click onto the **Pencil Tool** Hot Key **N**
- Alter the side seams and copy the selected body to the back Hot Key **Ctrl C, Ctrl B** Apple OS **Cmd C, Cmd B**
- Select the front body and alter the hem
- Select the back body and fill it with a gradient (refer to page 115 - changing the colour, direction and character of a gradient)
- Place the stitch and rib neck details onto the garment

Create The White Boarder Around The Tee Shirt:

- **Step 5:** This was achieved by selecting the back body, the sleeves and the neck band and by copying and moving these to the side - press the **Shift** and **Alt** keys at the same time as moving the selected shapes
- Do not deselect
- Click onto the **Add To Shape Area Tool** in **Pathfinder**
- Place a **Stroke** around the finished shape and increase the size of the stroke to approximately **6 pt's**
- **Step 6:** Place this shape behind the tee shirt and change the fill and stroke to white as this is going onto a black background
- **Step 7:** Marquee over the whole image and **Group** it Hot Key **Ctrl G** Apple OS **Cmd G**

Placement Print - Blue Tee Shirt:

- The placement print is made up of
  a. A traced photograph
  b. Figures traced with the **Pen Tool** over an image from the Internet
  c. Downloadable free fonts from a font web site and downloadable free **windings** from a font web site (refer to page 143)

- The blue tee shirt has an *Impact Print* on the front *An Impact Print is usually a 100% cover print, printed from edge to edge on a white ground*
- Mask the placement print with the front body shape

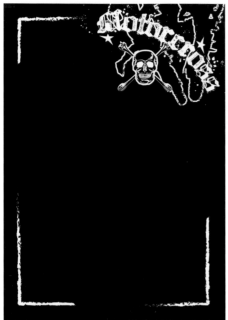

Layer 1 copy 1

Layered Story Board And Colour Changes:

- **Step 1:** Once the first tee shirt and placement print is finished, make a copy of that layer (refer to page 59)
- **Step 2:** Move the copied layer below Layer 1, by selecting it and holding the left mouse button down while dragging the layer down
- Click onto the eye (👁) next to Layer 1 to make the locked layer invisible
- **Step 3:** Create the background layer in this layer, using the placement print

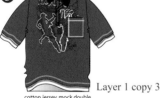

Layer 1

cotton jersey tee-shirt with
front placement print

Layer 1 copy 2

cotton jersey tee-shirt with
front impact placement print

Layer 1 copy 3

cotton jersey, mock double
poloshirt with coverstitch hems
& front placement print

- **Step 4: Tee shirt 2** was created adding to the placement print to create an Impact Print and changing colours, the tee shirt style is the same as Tee Shirt 1
- Copy Layer 1 again and lock Layer 1 and Layer 1 Copy 1
- You can now manipulate, ungroup and change colours in this new layer, refer to page 62 for steps
- The illustration demonstrates the steps to create this tee shirt
- The polo collar symbol was used to create this collar

- **Step 5: Tee shirt 3** was created using elements of the Impact Print and changing colours
- Copy Layer 1 again and lock Layer 1, Layer 1 Copy 1 and Layer 1 Copy 2
- You can now manipulate, ungroup and change colours in this new layer
- The illustration demonstrates the steps to create this tee shirt
- The polo collar symbol was used to create this collar

- Unlock all layers except the background layer (Layer 1 Copy 1) and arrange the tee shirts in place

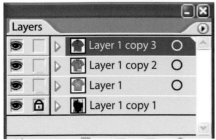

Layers

👁	☐	▷	👕 Layer 1 copy 3	○
👁	☐	▷	👕 Layer 1 copy 2	○
👁	☐	▷	👕 Layer 1	○
👁	🔒	▷	🖼 Layer 1 copy 1	

Downloading Fonts and Clipart:

- Downloading free fonts is very easy, however we would like to *WARN* you about the importance of familiarising yourself with copyright laws
- Generally, when you download a font a *Readme* file will be downloaded at the same time, click onto this file and it will give you the conditions of use for that particular font
- Wherever necessary, buying the font is preferable

Downloading A Font:

- **Step 1:** Open up your internet browser and search for **Fonts**
- There are a plethora of "free" font web sites - the one we find easy to navigate and always has good fonts is Dafont (www.dafont.com)
- Follow the web sites' instructions on viewing and downloading the font
- When downloading fonts from the internet ensure you select the correct file for your operating system
- The file extension or file name for a font is TTF
- The font will initially download in a compressed file format - this file will need *extracting*
- It is important to download the font to a folder where you will be able to locate it again - like a folder in your work folder for **Downloaded Fonts**

- **Step 2:**
  Instructions for PCs
  a: Open up Windows Explorer and go to your **Downloaded Fonts** folder, double click on the compressed file and you will be prompted to choose a program to extract the file
  b: The program will give you an option to extract the file to a certain folder - the font will need to be extracted to the Font folder in the WINDOWS OS folder for it to be activated as a font. The following is the path: **My Computer → C-Drive**

  WINDOWS
  Fonts

- The font will be filed under the font name

  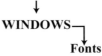

- You will be able to access it in the font list in **Adobe Illustrator** or in any other program on your computer

Downloading A Font:

Instructions for Mac OS X10.4.7
- Download the desired font to the Desktop
- Mac OS X will automatically expand it if it was a compressed file
- Double click on the folder to open the window
- Double click on the font
- This will automatically open **Font Book**
- **Font Book** now displays a preview of the font
- Click onto the **Install Font** button on the lower right side of the window
- A secondary **Font Book** window will open showing the new font file included in the list.
- Trash the original folder downloaded on the desktop.

Clip Art And Windings:

- **Clip art** comes in a variety of file formats from vector art through to Tiff Files - high quality bitmap files. Again it is important to take care with the copyright instructions here - most web sites or publications will stipulate how these can be used
- The following is a standard list - you must exercise caution when using clip art
1. You may use clip art in your school assignments and projects
2. You may use clip art in your church brochure
3. You may use clip art for personal, noncommercial uses
4. You may not use clip art to advertise your business
5. You may not use clip art to create a company logo
6. You may not use clip art to illustrate the chapters of a book

- **Windings** are font files, but they contain clip art images (refer to the Paisley on page 159)
- Windings are downloadable in the same way as fonts
- To use windings, it is important to type out the whole alphabet and **Create Outlines** (refer to page 116)
- The images will be grouped
- Ungroup the images to use individual images

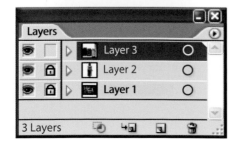

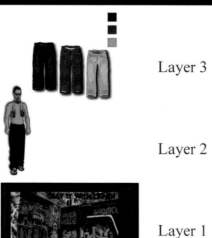

Layer 3

Layer 2

Layer 1

Creating Story Board 3: Men's Denim Jean Board

Story board 3 is made up of three layers

- **Layer 1:** Consists of the background photograph and the story board layout
- The background photograph is not edited and taken with a digital camera, opened up in Adobe Illustrator, placed on the page layout in landscape
- Remember to change the font to a vector image by selecting **Create Outlines** in the **Type** options when you save the final story board
- **Layer 2:** Consists of the croquis illustration. The croquis was developed from a photograph using the same principles as the first croquis you developed
- **Layer 3:** Consists of the styling - the looser more relaxed look was achieved by drawing the jeans onto a basic croquis (refer to page 99 for a male croquis) and loosening it up with the **Pencil Tool**

- The following pages will focus on how to achieve different washes and colours in denim

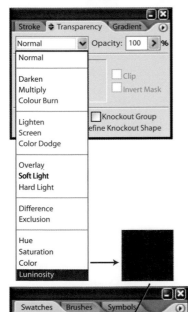

- Open up the reverse side denim scans from page 117 or scan another denim swatch
  This process requires a sharper contrast so it is best to use the reverse side of the denim

 a  b

- **Dark Wash:** This treatment uses swatch a with the following adjustments :

- **Step 1:** Draw a rectangle with a plain fill in it. This must be the depth of the colour you would like for the denim. Do not deselect this rectangle
- **Step 2:** Place the plain rectangle behind the denim scan Hot Key **Shift Ctrl [** Apple OS **Shift Cmd [**
- **Step 3:** Copy the rectangle to the back once more Hot Key **Ctrl C, Ctrl B** Apple OS **Cmd C, Cmd B** and remove the fill ( )

- **Step 4:** Select the denim only and go to the **Transparency** palette and select **Luminosity** (refer to page 127 for an explanation of **Luminosity)**

- Select the whole swatch and drag this into the **Swatches** palette
- Fill the illustration with the denim pattern fill

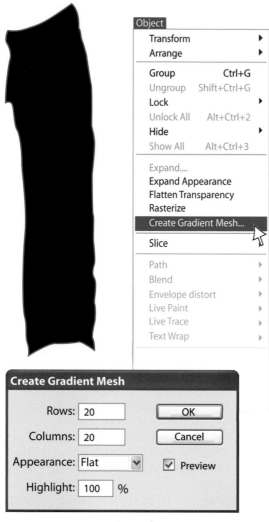

Object

Transform ▶
Arrange ▶

Group   Ctrl+G
Ungroup   Shift+Ctrl+G
Lock ▶
Unlock All   Alt+Ctrl+2
Hide ▶
Show All   Alt+Ctrl+3

Expand....
Expand Appearance
Flatten Transparency
Rasterize
Create Gradient Mesh...
Slice

Path ▶
Blend ▶
Envelope distort ▶
Live Paint ▶
Live Trace ▶
Text Wrap ▶

Create Gradient Mesh

Rows: `20`   [OK]
Columns: `20`   [Cancel]
Appearance: `Flat` ▾   ☑ Preview
Highlight: `100` %

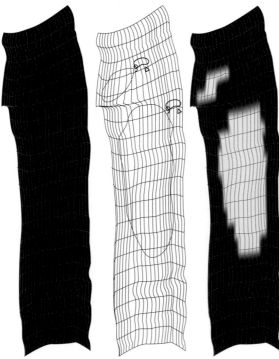

Create Gradient Mesh:

Lasso Tool Hot Key **Q**

*The wash effect in this jean was created using a **Gradient Mesh**. This tool has already been introduced in a simpler form on page 118, which suited the simpler shape of the shorts. For this more complex shape a more detailed **Gradient Mesh** is required so that you can have more control of where to place the highlights*

- **Step 1:** Copy each filled leg shape to the front
  Hot Key **Ctrl C, Ctrl F** Apple OS **Cmd C, Cmd F**
- Fill each of these shapes with a dark navy
- Go to **Object** in the menu, click onto **Create Gradient Mesh**

- An option box with rows and columns will appear
  More rows and columns in the image will give the option for more detailed shading but this will make your file much larger!!
- Type the number of rows and columns required in the option box
- Select the **Preview** option to see what the mesh will look like
- There is also a choice of **Appearance**
  Flat - gives the option to choose where you want to put the highlights - this is the option used on this jean
  To Centre - highlights the centre of the shape and
  To Edge - highlights the edges

- **Step 2:** Select the **Lasso Tool** Hot Key **Q**
- Go into the **Outline View** Hot Key **Ctrl Y**
  Apple OS **Cmd Y**
- Select the areas to be highlighted by tracing around the anchor points with the **Lasso Tool**
- Once these are highlighted - remember an active anchor point is a filled box and an inactive anchor point has a clear centre. Change the colour by selecting the highlight colour
- Yellow was used in this illustration to give the appearance of dirty denim
- Repeat this process for each of the shapes in the illustration
- There is no need to do this process with small pieces, like belt loops - here the same process that was demonstrated on page 118 can be used

Dark Wash   Medium Wash

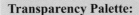

- **Step 1:** Select each of the shapes that have the gradient mesh in them
- **Step 2:** Go to the
  Transparency Palette
  ↓
  Multiply

  ⟶ **Opacity - 40%**
- The finished effect will look like dirty dark denim

This whole process is contingent on the paper and printer used. It is good to experiment and print out different colour combinations. You can then change colours and transparency accordingly

- The medium wash was achieved by changing the colours of the gradient mesh to grey and white
- Go to the **Transparency Palette**
  ↓
  Soft Light

  ⟶ **Opacity - 40%**
- Both of these finishes have used the denim swatch created on page 117

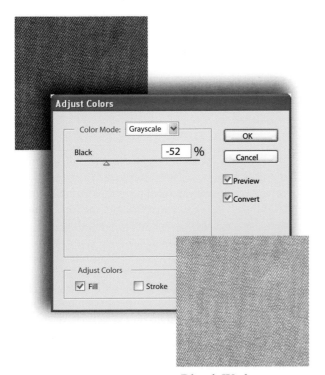

Bleach Wash

Grayscale And Adjusting Colours:

- **Step 1:** Select the scanned denim swatch and go to **Filter** in the menu bar
  ↓
  Colors ⟶ **Convert To Grayscale**
  Do not deselect

- **Step 2:** Go to **Filter** in the menu bar
  ↓
  Colors ⟶ **Adjust Colors...**

- Slide the arrow up and down the bar with the **Preview** box selected (☑) to achieve the correct depth of colour

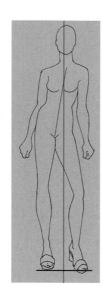

- The technique used to develop the female croquis is identical to those used for the male croquis, with two exceptions - the figure will be slender and more leggy

- As fashion changes, different areas of the body are emphasised
- For example: High heel shoes - longer legs
  Fur or roll collars - longer neck
  Padded shoulders - wider shoulders
- Whatever proportion is used, it is essential to draw in the **Balance Line**

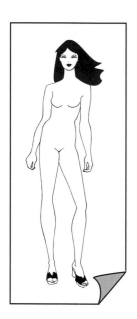
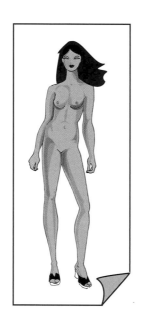

- Refer to pages 130 to 132

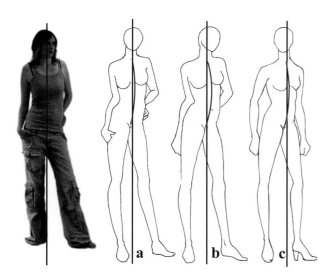

- You can add to your library of croquis by using your original croquis as a reference. The examples shown here are all identical proportions and slight variations to the movement through the torso. The main change is the leg positioning and thus the weight of the body changes.

  a: The weight-bearing foot is the closest to the **Balance Line** and in line with the **Pit of the Neck**
  b: The weight of the body is distributed between both feet with extra weight on the left ball of the foot.
  c: The weight of the body is evenly distributed between both feet

Creating Story Board 4:

Adobe Photoshop

Adobe Illustrator

- This story board is achieved using both **Adobe Illustrator** and **Adobe Photoshop**

- Each section is created as a separate file and then brought together in this composition as separate layers. This method is used due to the large size of the files

- *As in Adobe Illustrator, when using Adobe Photoshop there are varying methods which can be used to achieve the same end result. In Step 1 only, an alternative method is given.*

- **Layer 1:** Consists of the background photo taken with a digital camera and opened up in Adobe Illustrator
- The image is traced and changed from a bitmap image to a vector image.
- The Paisley pattern fill is created and applied as a block of colour
  Saved as: **Story Board 4 Fashion Illustration and Technical Drawing**

- **Layer 2:** Each technical drawing is created using information covered in the previous chapters
  Saved as: **Technical Drawing**

- **Layer 3:** Using the photo of the girl, the background is edited out using **Adobe Photoshop**. This is then placed onto a croquis which has been previously developed.
  Saved as: **Figure and garment**

As each file is completed in Adobe Illustrator, save as an individual file, copy and paste it into the ***Story board 4 Fashion Illustration and Technical Drawing*** *file*
Note: Before pasting, create a new layer each time

ADOBE PHOTOSHOP - WORK AREA

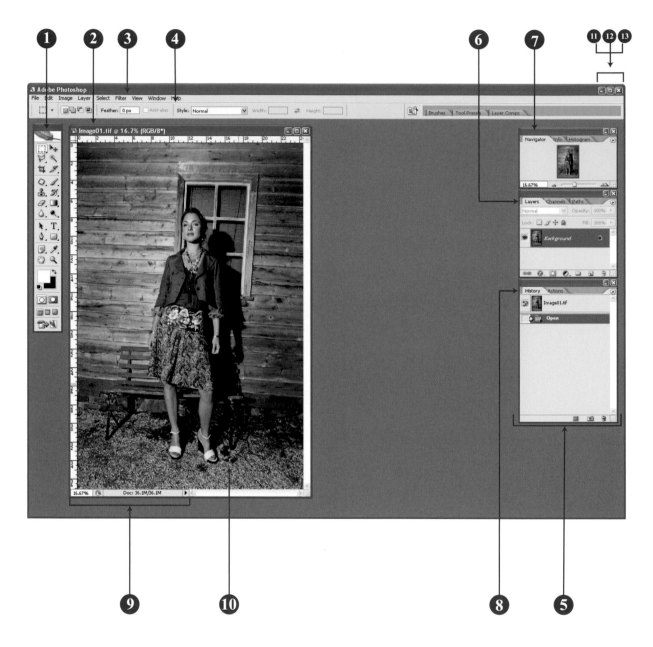

1 **Toolbox** - contains tools for creating and editing images.

2 **Title Bar** - the name of the file and the file type is displayed here

3 **Menu Bar** - contains menus organized by tasks.

4 **Option Bar** - provides options for using a tool.

5 **Palettes -** help you monitor and modify images. You can customise the palette locations in the workspace.

6 **Layers -** refer to page 151

7 **Navigator -** refer to page 151

8 **History -** refer to page 151

9 **Status Bar -** this is located at the bottom of every document window and displays useful information, such as the current magnification and file size of the active image

10 **Active Image Area** - displays the active open file. The window containing an open file is also called the **Document Window**

11 Minimise **12** Maximise **13** Close

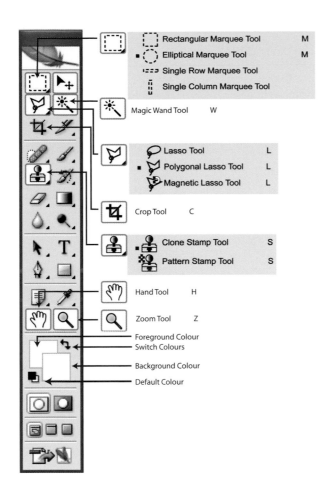

Rectangular Marquee Tool — M
Elliptical Marquee Tool — M
Single Row Marquee Tool
Single Column Marquee Tool

Magic Wand Tool — W

Lasso Tool — L
Polygonal Lasso Tool — L
Magnetic Lasso Tool — L

Crop Tool — C

Clone Stamp Tool — S
Pattern Stamp Tool — S

Hand Tool — H

Zoom Tool — Z

Foreground Colour
Switch Colours

Background Colour

Default Colour

Toolbox:

- **Rectangular Marquee** and **Elliptical Marquee** - allows you to draw a rectangle or an ellipse over the area you wish to select, to move, cut out or delete
  Single Row or **Single Column** - allows you to pick up a single row of horizontal pixels or a Single column of vertical pixels
- **Magic Wand** - selects continuous areas of colour, based on a Tolerance setting
- **Lasso** - allows you to use the cursor freehand as if you were drawing with a pen. This option works best with a stylus pen
- **Polygonal Lasso** - works by clicking onto the work area, moving the cursor and clicking again. Continue until you have defined the area you want to select. Click back at the start point to close the shape
- **Magnetic Lasso** - this option will stick to groups of similar colours and works best when there is a sharp contrast between the shape you want and other shapes or the background
- **Crop** - allows you to crop unwanted areas of an image and reduce the file size
- **Clone Stamp** - allows you to copy part of an image and apply it to another part of the image at the same time
- **Pattern Stamp** - allows you to paint with a pattern. A pattern can be selected from the pattern libraries or can be created
- **Hand** - use the Hand Tool in addition to using the scroll bars to move around the image
- **Zoom** - allows zooming in and out of your image
- **Navigator**
  You can drag the zoom slider to the right to zoom in, or to the left to zoom out. Each time you change the zoom level, the view in the Preview area updates
  Drag the red View box in the Preview area to move quickly to different areas of the image
- **Layers**
  Layers allows you to keep various images separate so that you can make changes without deleting or changing the underlying pixels. Each additional layer you create increases the file size of the image.
- **History**
  Every time you modify your image this is recorded in the **History** palette as a history state. The **History** palette records the last 20 states of the image. To delete a **History** state, drag the state into the **Waste Basket** icon at the bottom of the palette

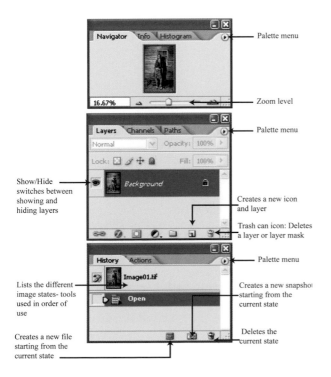

Palette menu

Zoom level

Palette menu

Show/Hide switches between showing and hiding layers

Creates a new icon and layer

Trash can icon: Deletes a layer or layer mask

Palette menu

Lists the different image states- tools used in order of use

Creates a new snapshot starting from the current state

Creates a new file starting from the current state

Deletes the current state

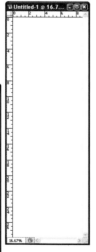

Method 1

Method 1:

Rectangle Marquee Tool Hot Key **M**

- **Step 1:** Open the JPEG or TIFF file from the digital camera
- Click onto the **Rectangular Marquee Tool** Hot Key **M** and drag across the area you want to frame

- **Step 2:** Click onto **Edit** in the menu bar
  ↓
  Copy Hot Key Ctrl **C**

- **Step 3:** Go to **File** in the menu bar
  ↓
  New (*do not change any of the details*)
- **OK**

- **Step 4:** Click onto **Edit** again and select **Paste** Hot Key Ctrl **V** Apple OS **Cmd V**
- **File**
- **Save As** Hot Key **Shift Ctrl S** Apple OS **Shift Cmd S**
- Name the new file " **Edited Garment"**
- Close the original photograph

Method 2:

Crop Tool Hot Key **C**

- **Step 1:** Open the JPEG or TIFF file from the digital camera
- Immediately make a copy of the file by going to the menu bar and select **Image Duplicate**
- Close the original file
- **Step 2:** Click onto **Crop Tool** Hot Key **C** and drag across the area you want to frame
- Double click on the image
- **File**
- **Save As** Hot Key **Shift Ctrl S** Apple OS **Shift Cmd S**
- Name the new file " **Edited Garment"**

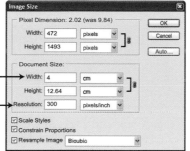

Image Reduction And Editing:

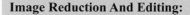

Rectangle Marquee Tool Hot Key **M**

- **Step 1:** Maximise the screen ()
- Reduce the size of the image considering the composition of the story board
- Go to **Image** in the menu bar

   Image Size Hot Key **Alt Ctrl I**
   ↓
   Document Size e.g. Width 4 cm → **OK**

- **Step 2:** Make certain that the **Foreground Colour** and the **Background Colours** are both **White.** Bring the swatch box to be changed to the front Hot Key **X** to bring the black to the front (■) and select white (□) from the **Swatches** palette
- Click onto the **Rectangular Marquee Tool** Hot Key **M** and drag across the area you want to delete. Press the delete key as each section is edited

Edit Image: Clone Stamp Tool

Zoom Tool Hot Key **Z**
Clone Stamp Tool Hot Key **S**

- **Step 3:** To remove the jewellery from the blouse, click onto the **Zoom Tool** Hot Key **Z** to enlarge the image
- Click onto the **Clone Stamp Tool** Hot Key **S** (refer to page 151)
- Set the brush size using the palette in the Options Bar
- Make certain that the **Aligned** option is selected

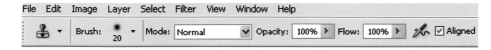

- Hold down the **Alt** key and click onto the part of the image you want to clone. Release the **Alt** key and then move the cursor to the area to be replaced
- To re-anchor the clone point, place the cursor over the new area you want to clone, hold down the **Alt** key and click
- Repeat these steps until the cloning is complete

- **Step 4:** To edit out the background leaving only the garment in place, click onto the **Polygon Lasso Tool** Hot Key **L** (this is the easiest of the three **Lasso Tool** options to control)
- Select **Anti-alias (☑)** in the Options Bar.
- Make certain that the **Feather** option is set on **0 px**

- Position the cursor outside the image in the grey area and click. Move the cursor and click, continuing on until you have defined the area you want to select, ending up back where you started to complete the selection. You will recognise when you are over the beginning by the circle next to the **Polygon Lasso** icon (▽) As each section is completed press the **Delete** key
  Start off with small areas until you become familiar with the technique
- Pressing Hot Key Ctrl **D** Apple OS **Cmd D** will deselect a selected area
  *If you make a mistake or want to alter a shape go to the **History** palette.*

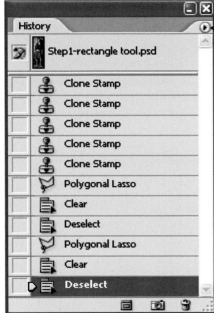

- The **History** palette has the same effect as the Hot Key Ctrl **Z** Apple OS **Cmd Z** (undo an action) in Adobe Illustrator
- It shows all past actions and gives you the opportunity to go back to a certain point, or back to the original file that you opened. By default the **History** palette records the last 20 steps
- **To delete a step**: click onto the step and drag it into the **Waste Basket** icon
- **To clear a step:** click onto the **Palette Menu** option and select **Clear History.** All recorded steps will be deleted from the **History** palette, leaving the image at the most recent stage

  *If the original image had a white background, the **Magic Wand Tool** would be the preferred tool as it selects continuous areas of colour, based on tolerance setting*

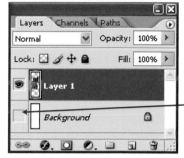

Layers in Adobe Photoshop:

*Layers in Adobe Photoshop perform in a similar way as in Adobe Illustrator. The first time you open an image in Adobe Photoshop it will default to a layer called Background. In this exercise, because the image has been copied and pasted into a new file, the background layer is white and the image when pasted becomes **Layer 1***

- **Step 1:** It is essential to hide the Background layer by clicking onto the **Eye (👁)** icon next to **Background** in the **Layers** palctte, to make this layer invisible when you open the file in Adobe Illustrator

- The background will appear as a grey check pattern when this layer is hidden

Save the image as a **PSD** file and name the file: **Edited Garment**

- Close Adobe Photoshop

Adobe
Illustrator CS2

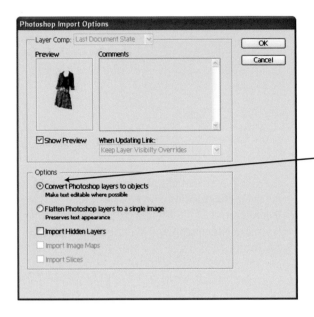

PSD File Opened In Adobe Illustrator:

- **Step 2:** Open **Adobe Illustrator**
- Open up the file saved in **Adobe Photoshop**

  ↓

  Edited garment. PSD

- Click onto **Convert Photoshop layers to objects**
- **OK**

- **Step 3:** Draw a coloured rectangle over the top of the garment.

- Send this to the back of the garment, allowing you to check that the background is transparent
- Once checked, delete the rectangle and save it as a Adobe Illustrator file **Edited garment.ai**

- Click onto the garment and
  Copy Hot Key **Crtl C** Apple OS **Cmd C**

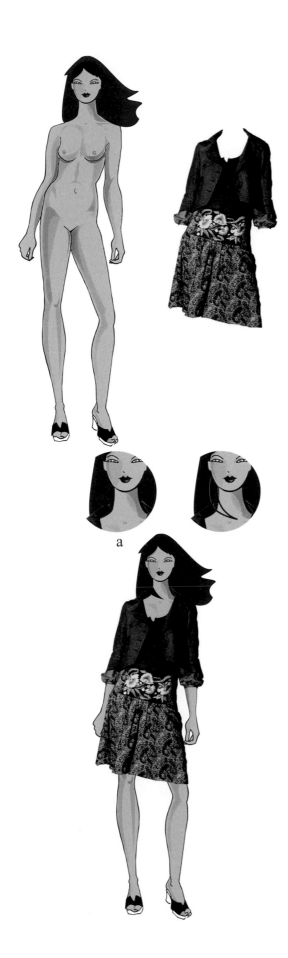

a

Female Croquis and Edited Garments:

- **Step 4:** Open up the file **Female Croquis Library** and select the female figure that was drawn from this photo
- Save it with a new file name: **Figure And Garment**

- **Paste** Hot Key **V** the garment into the file and position it onto the figure

- When drawing the female croquis the neck is made slimmer and longer. Because of this, the garment will sit away from the neck as illustrated in **a**. In this instance a shape has been drawn over the collar forming a part of the hair

!REMEMBER!
Zoom For Details

- Click onto the **Selection Tool** Hot Key **V,** marquee over the whole image and **Group** Hot Key **G**

- **Step 5: Save** Hot Key **Ctrl S** Apple OS **Cmd S**

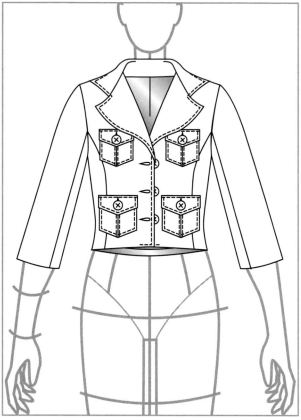

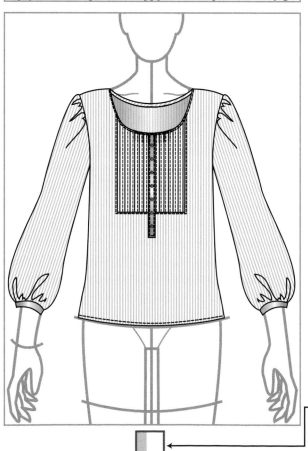

Black And White Garments With Improvised Fabric Fills:

Pen Tool Hot Key **P**

Use the Croquis on page 99 as a template to draw the styles
Save as: **Technical Drawing**

Jacket:

There are no features in the jacket that have not been covered in previous chapters. A list of operations featured in the jacket are as follows:

- **Step 1:** The **Pen Tool** was used to create the jacket. The right half was drawn first including the sleeve, stitch details and half the collar, and then it was reflected to create the left half. The buttons on the opening were changed to buttonholes and the collar was joined at the centre back and **Sent Backwards** Hot Key **Shift [** Apple OS **Cmd [** to sit behind the lapel
  Remember to always create closed shapes even when you are working in black and white
- **Step 2:** The back view has a **Gradient Fill** to give the illusion of depth

Shirt:

The shirt has pin tucks, satin cuffs and button stand and the fabric is a shadow stripe

- **Step 1:** The satin cuffs and button stand were achieved using a **Gradient Fill**
- **Step 2:** The pin tucks are a pattern brush created with a dashed line and a solid line

- Place the first pin tuck next to the button stand and copy it six times towards the yoke edge
- Place the first and last tucks in position
- Select all the tucks. Distribute the spacing between the tucks with the **Horizontal Distribute Centre Tool** ( )
- **Group** the tucks and reflect copy them to the opposite side
- Mask the tucks with the yoke, select the edge of the yoke with the **Group Selection Tool** and put a white fill and black stroke into it
- **Step 3:** The shadow stripe is a simple vertical stripe pattern repeat. The stripe pattern repeat in the sleeves is rotated using the **Tilda** key (refer to page 110)

abcdefghijklmno

pqrstuvwxyz

20mm

20mm

- **Step 1:** The pattern repeat in the skirt was achieved by using downloadable free fonts from the Internet
- The paisley pattern is a font
- Type out the whole alphabet and select the **Paisley** font from the **Font** library and **Create Outlines** (refer to page 92)
- Ungroup the designs and select the designs you wish to use - **Delete** the rest
- **Step 2:** Create a 20mm square rectangle and create the repeat (refer to pages 56-57)
- Even though there are now three icons the same principles still apply

Remember to always copy across what happens on the edges of the repeat

Note the icons in the same colours

- **Step 3:** Fill the skirt with the pattern repeat and scale the design to suit the size of the sketch (refer to page 58)
- **Step 4:** This style has a contrast front basque panel. This has been achieved by scaling the pattern repeat up to about 200%

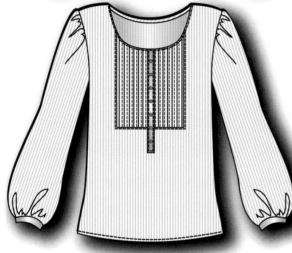

Drop Shadows:

- Once all three styles have been drawn up you can create a drop shadow
- **Step 1:** Group each garment individually
- **Step 2:** Go to **Filter** in the menu bar

    ↓

    Stylise

    ⟶ **Drop Shadow**

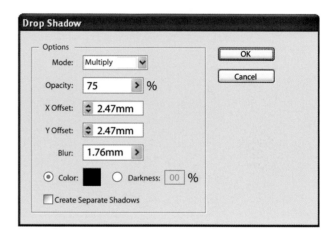

- **Mode:** This works the same way as in the **Transparency** palette
- **Opacity:** The depth of the colour
- **X Offset:** This is the horizontal offset ie: how far up or down the shadow is placed
- **Y Offset:** This is the vertical offset ie: how far left or right the shadow is placed
  In this example the shadow will fall to the left and down, if a subtraction symbol had been placed next to the numbers the shadow would have fallen to the left and up
- **Blur:** This controls the blurring on the edge of the shadow
- **Color:** The colour of the shadow can be changed by double clicking onto the color box and an option to change the colour will appear
- **Create Separate Shadows:** When this is ticked each part of the illustration will have a visible shadow, when it is not ticked only the combined shadow will be visible
-

!REMEMBER!
*Save the file Hotkey **Ctrl S** Apple OS **Cmd S***

This file will be copied and pasted into the background file. Do not forget to create a new layer in the background file before you paste this image down

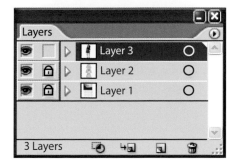

- **Step 1:** Open the file containing your digital photographs JPEG or TIFF. The image may be much larger than the A4 page and also a large file size. To reduce the file size **Export** and make certain that the file type is a **JPEG.** Save it as a **CMYK, CUSTOM 150dpi** and save it as a new name: **Story Board 4 Fashion Illustration and Technical Drawing**, so as not to confuse the two files. Close the original file and open up the new file. Save it again as an Illustrator file: **Fashion Illustration and Technical Drawing.ai**
  This is the main file for Story Board 4
- **Step 2:** Select the image which is a bitmap image and click onto the arrow next to **Live Trace** in the menu bar

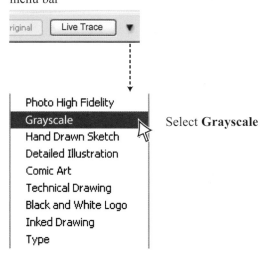

Select **Grayscale**

- Once the image is traced, an option to **Expand** the image will appear in the tool bar

- Click onto this option and the image will become a vector image
- Deselect the image
- **Step 3:** Scale to fit the page considering planned layout
- If necessary mask the area needed. Create a rectangle, the size that you want to mask. Marquee over the rectangle and image, right click the mouse **Make Clipping Mask**
- **Step 4:** Using the **Rectangle Tool** create a square and fill it with the **Paisley Print** created for the skirt
- **Step 5**: Arrange both the photo and Paisley square on the page considering final layout
  Layer 1 (refer to page 149)

Layer 1

Layer 2

Layer 3

Creating Story Board 5

- **Story Board 5** is made up of three layers

- **Layer 1:** Consists of the background photo taken with a digital camera and opened up in Illustrator. The colour is changed to grey tones and colour applied

- **Layer 2:** Using the photo of the girl changed to Grayscale, traced and colour applied. The garment is outlined and masked. This is then placed onto a croquis which had been previously developed

- **Layer 3:** Colour swatches, Text, Original Photo and Masked details

17-4440 TP

16-6329 TP

18-4432 TP

19-4671 TP

Digital Photo: Bitmap Image Changed To A Vector Image, Grayscale And Colour Applied

- **Step 1:** Refer to page 161, Step 1 and Step 2

- **Step 2:** Scale the image to fit the page considering the planned layout. If necessary distort (reduce the width). This image does not contain any figures
- Select the **Group Selection Tool**
- Go to **Windows Swatch Libraries**
  ↓
  Default CMYK
- Fill each section with the desired colours
- **Step 3:** If necessary **Mask** the area needed. Create a **Rectangle** Hot Key **M** the size that you want to mask. Marquee over the rectangle and image, right click the mouse **Make Clipping Mask**
- Save as: **Story Board 5 - Blue Lady**

Scan Photo, Place In Illustrator And Trace:

- **Step 1:** Create a new Layer (Layer 2) following directions outlined on pages 33 and 34
- Lock Layer 1 in the **Layers** palette
- **Step 2:** Scan the photo of the girl, change the colour mode to **Grayscale** and **150 dpi** in the scanner options
- **Step 3:** Save as a JPEG file: **Grey Lady. JPEG**
- **Step 4:** Place the file into **Adobe Illustrator** (refer to page 31)
- **Step 5:** Select the image which is a bitmap image and click onto the arrow next to **Live Trace** in the menu bar

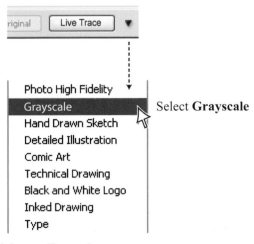

Select **Grayscale**

- Click onto **Expand**
- Click onto this option and the image will become a vector image

Edit Garment And Stylise The Female Croquis:

Magic Wand Tool Hot Key **Y**
Pen Tool Hot Key **P**
Selection Tool Hot Key **V**

- **Step 6:** Select the **Magic Wand Tool** Hot Key **Y** and click onto a shape, the Magic Wand Tool selects objects with similar colours depending on the tolerance
- Change the tolerance level by double clicking onto the icon in the Toolbox, an option box will appear. Set the tolerance to **20** to capture any other shapes within 20% of the colour of the first shape selected as this example demonstrates
- Fill each section with the desired colours

Unlike the previous technique used, shapes will be randomly selected

- **Step 7:** Draw a closed shape around the area you want to mask with the **Pen Tool** Hot Key **P**
- **Step 8:** Deselect, then click onto the **Selection Tool** Hot Key **V**. Marquee over the shape and image, right click the mouse, select **Make Clipping Mask**

- **Step 9:** From the croquis developed, select the one drawn from this photograph. Make any changes to the croquis at this stage, for example shoes and hair
- The strands of hair are drawn using the **Pen Tool** Hot Key **P**. Draw the first and last strands and blend the strands to achieve the same effect as the illustration. Select the **Blend Tool** Hot Key **W** and click onto one strand/line then the other (refer to page 139 - Step 3)

- **Step 10:** Position the masked garment over the top of the nude figure
- Deselect
- Click onto the **Selection Tool** Hot Key **V** and marquee over the whole figure, right click and group

!REMEMBER!
*Save the file Hotkey **Ctrl S** Apple OS **Cmd S***

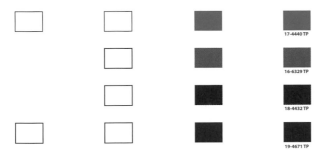

17-4440 TP

16-6329 TP

18-4432 TP

19-4671 TP

Colour Swatches And Identity Numbers:

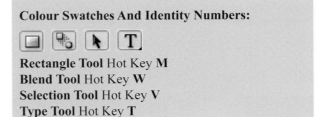

Rectangle Tool Hot Key **M**
Blend Tool Hot Key **W**
Selection Tool Hot Key **V**
Type Tool Hot Key **T**

- **Step 1:** Create a new layer (**Layer 3**) following directions on pages 33 and 34
- Lock **Layer 2** in the **Layers** palette
- **Step 2:** Colour Swatches (refer to page 139)
- **Step 3:** Type in the colour name or number of each swatch

Grayscale Image: Details Highlighted

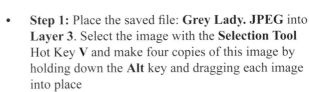

Selection Tool Hot Key **V**
Rectangle Tool Hot Key **M**

- **Step 1:** Place the saved file: **Grey Lady. JPEG** into **Layer 3**. Select the image with the **Selection Tool** Hot Key **V** and make four copies of this image by holding down the **Alt** key and dragging each image into place
- Do not alter the first image

- **Step 2:** Select different areas of the second, third and fourth image that you want to emphasise by drawing rectangles over the image with the **Rectangle Tool** Hot Key **M** as illustrated

- **Step 3:** Marquee over each image and shape individually, right click the mouse **Make Clipping Mask**

Composition:

- Unlock all layers, arrange and scale as needed. When satisfied with the balance of the composition, lock that layer

!REMEMBER!
*Save the file Hotkey **Ctrl S** Apple OS **Cmd S***

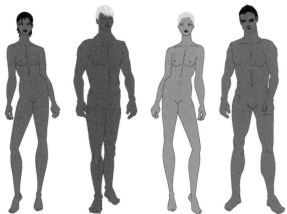

Story Board 6 - Chef Wear Corporate:

- This story board consists of four figures based on the hand drawn illustrations, developed earlier in the chapter

- An embroidered logo

- A simple check repeat - follow instructions for a simple pattern repeat

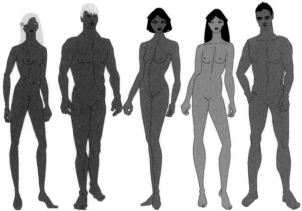

Story Board 7 - Club Aloha Corporate:

- This story board consists of five figures based on the hand drawn illustrations, developed earlier in the chapter

- A logo, which can also be used in the pattern swatch for the neck tie

- A more complex pattern swatch which uses all the same principles as the Broderie Anglaise design in chapter 3

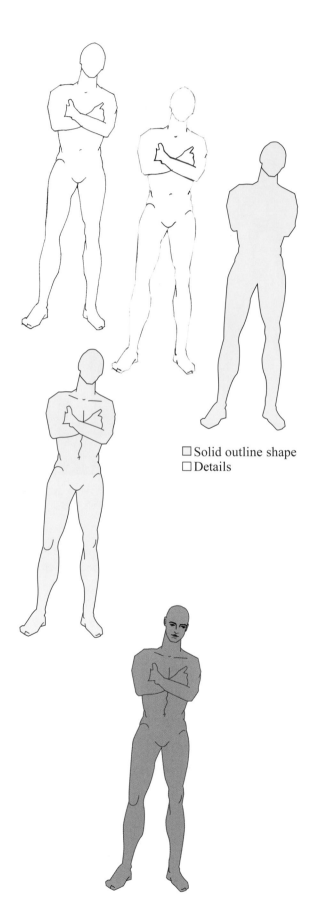

□ Solid outline shape
□ Details

Drawing Over A Scanned Figure:

Selection Tool Hot Key **V**
Direct Selection Tool Hot Key **A**
Pen Tool Hot Key **P**
Scissors Tool Hot Key **C**

• **Step 1:** Open the scanned images of the croquis you have created. Trace over each one with the **Pen Tool** Hot Key **P**

It is important to draw around the perimeter of the croquis, to create a solid closed shape and then fill in the line detail

• **Step 2:** Add the facial features to the croquis

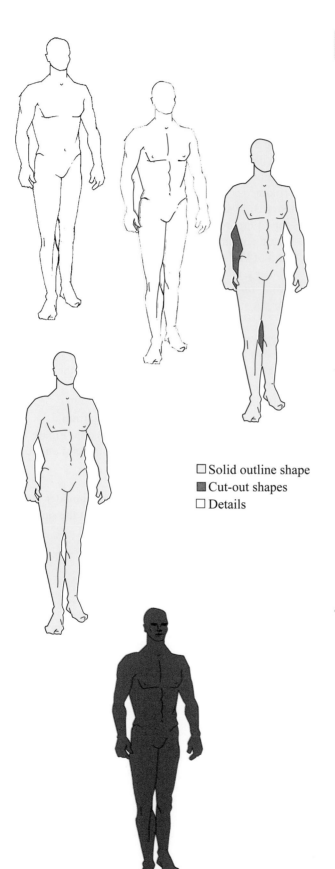

- **Step 3:** This croquis is different to the first croquis, as it has areas that need to be cut out
- Draw around the perimeter of the figure

- Draw in the cut-out shape details

- Draw in the line details

- Select the solid perimeter shape and the cut-out shapes
- Go to the **Pathfinder** palette and select the **Divide Tool** ( )

- **Delete** all of the cut-out sections

- **Step 4:** Add the facial features to the croquis

☐ Solid outline shape
■ Cut-out shapes
☐ Details

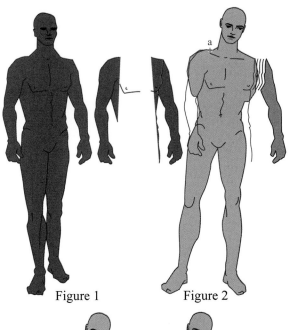

Figure 1   Figure 2

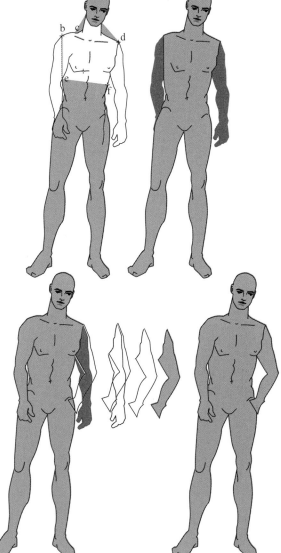

Changing The Computer Figure:

- **Step 1:** Make a copy of both figures
  Hot Key **Ctrl C**, **Ctrl V**
  Apple OS **Cmd C**, **Cmd V**
- **Step 2:** Delete most of Figure 1 except for the arms and the Pectoral muscles
- Remove the **Fill** and make the **Stroke** a contrasting colour
- **Step 3:** Place the arms and the pectoral muscles on top of Figure 2
- Cut the right shoulder of Figure 2 where the right arm of Figure 1 joins a
- Create a closed shape with the left arm of the figure
  Note: the pectoral muscle shape has been used to do this

- **Step 4:** Delete the parts of Figure 2 that will not be used in the re-created figure
- Cut the shoulder of the right arm where the body will be turned into a closed shape b
- Join the shoulder at c
- Rotate the left arm and the side body from d
- Cut the side body at f where it joins onto Figure 1
- Delete the part of the line below that point and join Figure 1 to f
- Join b and e
- Move the left arm aside and join the shoulder at d
- Bring the right arm to the front and put the same **Fill** and **Stroke** as Figure 1 into it

- **Step 5:** Draw a folded arm going into a pocket on the left side using the left arm as a guide

- Delete all of the left arm except the pectoral muscle and use this to close the arm shape

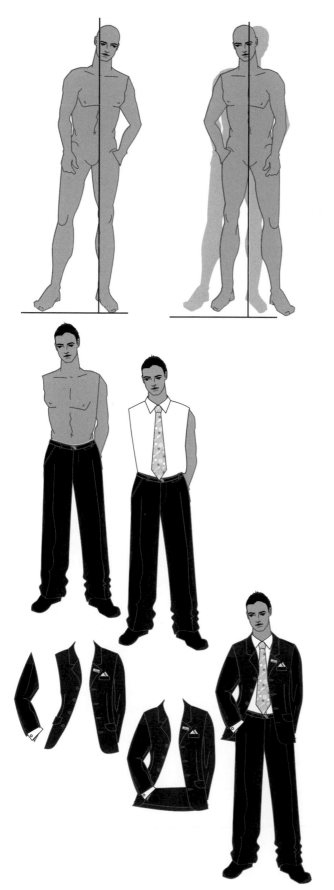

Reflect Pose:

- Reflect the finished figure and rotate the figure on the vertical **Balance Line** from the **Pit of the Neck** to correct the weight of the figure
  Note: it is helpful to keep the balance line, as demonstrated on pages 130-132, throughout the drawing, as it helps with the balance of the figure

Dress the Figure:

- **Step 1:** Move his right arm aside and dress the figure going from the items furthest back to the items in front

  Remember, when drawing in Adobe Illustrator, the first thing you draw is furthest back in the layering of objects order

  a: Draw the shoes first
  b: The trousers
  c: The shirt using the trousers as a guide
  d: Bring the trousers in front of the shirt and then draw the tie
  e: Draw the front jacket including the left sleeve
  f: Draw the back of the jacket, using the front of the jacket as a guide, group the front jacket and left sleeve - do not include the back
  g: Send the back of the jacket behind the figure
  h: The last item to draw will be the right sleeve, using the right arm as a guide. Group all of these so that the arm is included with the sleeve and the hand is visible when placing the sleeve onto the figure

- **Step 2:** Marquee over the whole figure and group it

TOMBOY

lime/white   black/white   red/white

Story Board 8 - Lingerie With Stylised Croquis:

- This story board consists of a figure based on the hand drawn illustrations, developed earlier in this chapter

- A simple two colour stripe (refer to page 108)

- Front and back views of a camisole and knickers using the female croquis on page 99 as a guide

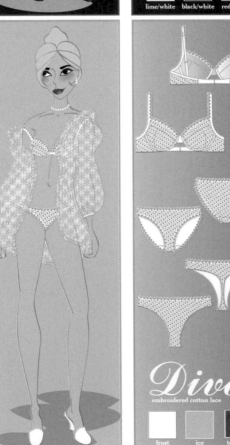

Diva
embroidered cotton lace

frost   ice   tearose

Story Board 9 - Lingerie With Stylised Croquis:

- This story board consists of a figure based on the hand drawn illustrations, developed earlier in this chapter

- An embroidered fabric using a repeat section of the Broderie Anglaise developed in Chapter 4

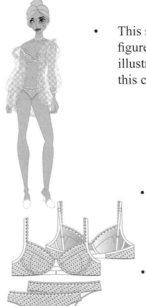

- Front and back views of a brassiere and two pairs of knickers, using the female croquis on page 99 as a guide

!REMEMBER!
Zoom For Details

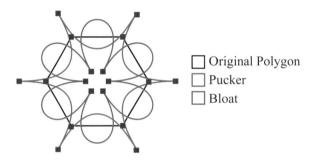

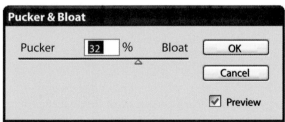

☐ Original Polygon
☐ Pucker
☐ Bloat

Pucker & Bloat

Pucker [32] % Bloat

OK

Cancel

☑ Preview

Embroidered Fabric Pattern Swatch:

Selection Tool Hot Key **V**
Direct Selection Tool Hot Key **A**

- **Step 1:** Open the Broderie Anglaise fabric you created (refer to Chapter 3), and copy the full repeat into a new file
- Delete everything except the small flower and dot pattern
- Scale the square background rectangle to fit the repeat
- Use the top left corner and the right bottom corner as guides
- Create a pattern swatch
- **Step 2:** Copy the Broderie Anglaise scalloped brush stroke you created into the new file

Flower Fabric Pattern Swatch:

Polygon Tool No Hot Key
Selection Tool Hot Key **V**

- **Step 1: Creating a six petal flower with the Pucker and Bloat Tool:**
  Create a six sided **Polygon** (refer to page 9)
  Do not deselect the **Polygon**
- Go to **Filter** in the menu bar
  ↓
  Distort

  ⟶**Pucker & Bloat**

- Move the arrow to the left, to **Bloat** the polygon

  Bloat: *Pulls the polygon's anchor points inward while curving the sides outward, creating a flower shape*
  Pucker: *Pulls the polygon's anchor points outward while curving the sides inward, creating a star shape*
  Both options pull the anchor points relative to the polygon's centre point.

- **Step 2:** Create a pattern repeat (refer to page 56)

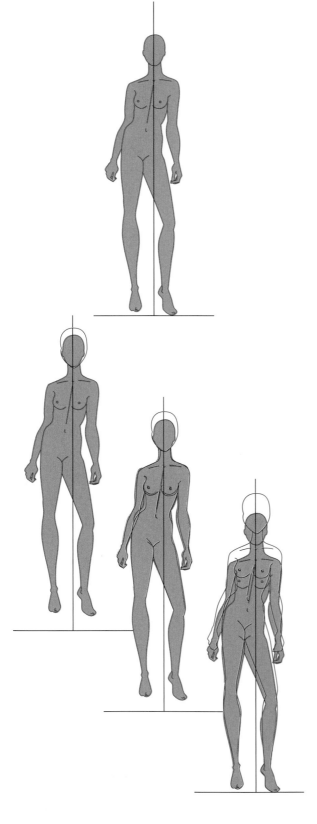

Creating A Cartoon Figure:

Selection Tool Hot Key **V**
Direct Selection Tool Hot Key **A**
Pen Tool Hot Key **P**
Scissors Tool Hot Key **C**

- **Step 1:** Copy one of the female croquis you have created into a new file
- **Step 2:** Draw in the vertical balance line through the pit of the neck and a horizontal base line

This figure will be developed in the same way as created in the first croquis, making it even more exaggerated, as the base figure is already stylised

- **Step 3:** Draw the head. A slightly larger head gives the figure more of a cartoon look

- **Step 4:** Draw in the neck - note it is slightly thinner

- **Step 5:** Draw in the shoulders and the rest of the figure to the knees (similar to the hand-drawn original croquis)

Note the exaggerated pinched waist and rounder breasts. These details are determined by the end use as well as your own style of drawing

- **Step 6:** Move the balance line and the croquis down about half a head and draw in the feet

- **Step 7:** Join the feet to the knees

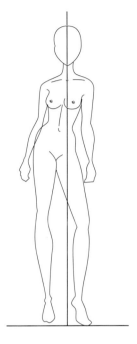

Creating A Cartoon Figure Continued:

- **Step 8:** Once the figure is complete remove the original figure

Creating Realistic Looking Hands And Feet By Tracing Over The Original Photograph:

One of the most common difficulties is drawing hands and feet. To circumvent this you can draw over a photograph

- **Step 1:** Copy the photograph you used to create the croquis
- Lock the photograph Hot Key **Ctrl 2** Apple OS **Cmd 2**
- Zoom up very close to the hands and draw over the hands with the pen tool

- **Step 2:** Repeat this with the feet

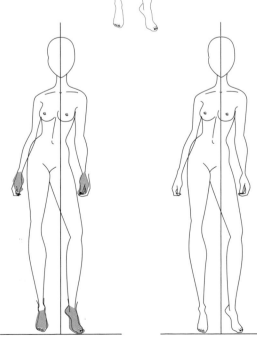

- **Step 3:** Place the new hands and feet in position over the drawing
- **Step 4:** Cut off the hands and feet of the original drawing
- **Step 5:** Adjust the new hands and feet until they look well proportioned to the figure and join them to the body (refer to page 37 **Average** and **Join**)
- The line drawing is complete

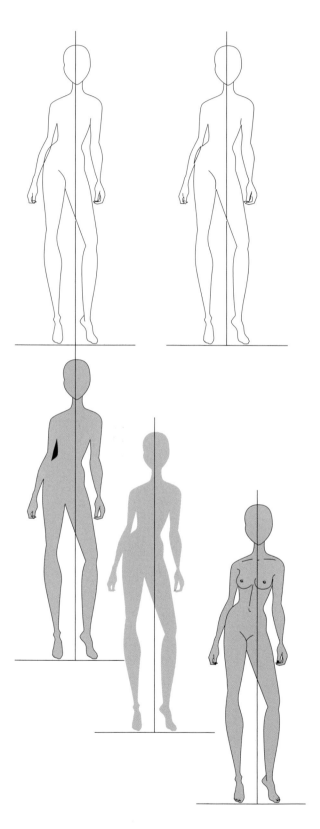

Creating A Cartoon Figure: Silhouette

- **Step 1:** Make a copy of the figures
  Hot Key **Ctrl C**, **Ctrl V**
  Apple OS **Cmd C**, **Cmd V**

- **Step 2:** Delete all of the details as in the first figure

- **Step 3:** Cut the lines either side of the intersections - see the grey line in the illustration

- **Step 4:** Join all open ends, where the hip joins the arm, the left underarm of the figure and the crotch

- **Step 5:** Once these are all joined you will now have a closed shape
- Select the shape between the right torso and arm and the figure shape excluding the head and divide the shapes with the **Divide Tool** in the **Pathfinder** palette( )

- **Step 6:** Delete the cut-out shape
- Remove the stroke

Creating A Cartoon Figure: Completed

- **Step 7:** Put the line details over the top of the drawing to complete it. Marquee and group it

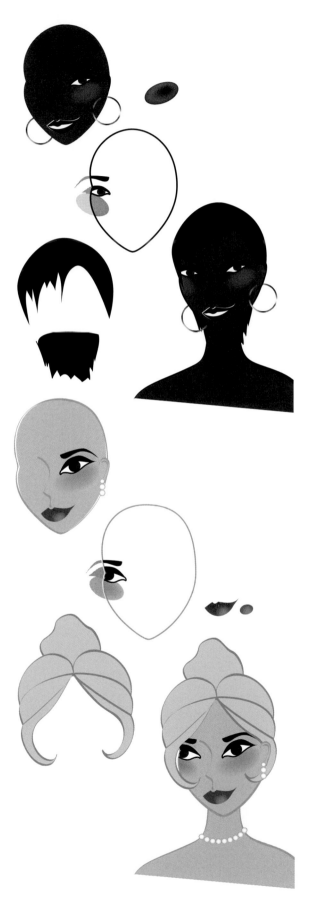

Creating A Cartoon Figure: Face and Hair

- **Step 1:** Draw in the facial features for the head in **story board 8** This head is not as big as the head in story board 9. This is all a matter of personal style and end use

- **Step 2:** The blush on the cheek was achieved by drawing an ellipse and using the **Mesh Tool** to put a colour into the ellipse (refer to page 118). It was then put in place and made transparent so as not to look so harsh

- **Step 3:** The right eye of the face was achieved by **Reflect** copying the left eye, moving the eyeball over and masking the eye and blush on the cheek with the shape of the face

- **Step 4:** The hair was drawn with the **Pencil Tool** in two parts - the shape on top of the head and the shape behind the neck

- **Step 5:** The hooped earrings were drawn with the **Ellipse Tool** using a **2 pt** stroke, cut to look like they are attached to an ear lobe and then the stroke was turned into an outline (refer to page 105 **Outline Stroke**). The earrings were then filled with a **Gradient** fill

This face was achieved using the same processes, the only difference being the lips. The lips have a spot of shine on them, created the same way as the blush on the cheek

The Internet has become a very important source of reference in the Fashion Industry. Fashion Designers and Product Developers are able to research and analyse the latest trends the instant they hit the public domain world wide. Students in Universities and Colleges have grown up with this technology and are very adept at surfing the web. Used correctly the web can be inspirational and informative, showing the next trends, newest fabrics available, the latest hardware and software and even the success or otherwise of your competitor.

Web sites have become the showcase for leading fashion designers, clothing companies and fashion magazines to advertise and display their wares. For this reason we have not given an endless list of these, you only have to go to one of the search engines and type in a name. Web sites also come and go but we would hope that those listed survive and are of assistance to you.

Free Web Sites

- **General:**

  www.wwd.com/dictionary/fashion
  www.rivers.com.au/links/fashion_publications.htm
  www.rivers.com.au/links/designer_fashion.htm
  www.wgsn.com/edu (free to education institutions)
  www.fashion-era.com
  www.ciff.dk

- **Catwalk Parades And Collections:**

  www.style.com
  www.fashion.net/sites/fashion/
  www.missixty.com

- **Trend Books:**

  www.sachapacha.com
  www.mudpie.co.uk/index.htm
  www.dressing-magazine.com

- **Fashion Magazines:**

  www.elle.com
  www.glamourmagazine
  www.harpersbazaar.com
  www.marieclaire.com
  www.vogue.com
  www.killah.it

- **Fashion Illustrations, Graphics And Technical Drawings:**

  www.meannorth.com/FASHIONFICTION2.htm
  www.jaspergoodall.com
  www.catecoles.co.uk/
  www.bettiblue.com
  www.fashioninformation.com/fix/300902.htm
  www.kschung.com
  www.acidtwist.com/
  www.ufho.com/images

- **Computer Web Sites:**

  www.adobe.com

- **Subscription Web Sites:**

  www.wgsn.com
  www.fernmitchell.com/FashionLinks.php

Text books

- **Computer:**

  Skintik, Catherine, *Learning Adobe Illustrator CS2*, Pearson Hall
  YoungJin.com *Illustrator CS Accelerated, YJ IT Publishing Team*
  Aldrich, Winifred, *CAD in Clothing and Textiles*, Blackwell Science
  Tallon, Kevin, *Creative Fashion Design with Illustrator*, Batsford
  Burke, Sandra, *Fashion Computing Design Techniques and CAD*, Burke Publishing

- **Fashion Illustration and Drawing:**

  Borelli, Laird, *Fashion Illustration Now*, Thames & Hudson
  Borelli, Laird, *Fashion Illustration Next*, Thames & Hudson
  Hagen, Kathryn, *Illustration for Designers*, Prentice Hall
  McKelvey, Kathryn, *Fashion Source Book*, Blackwell Publishing
  Taham, Caroline & Seaman, Julian, *Fashion Design Drawing Course*, Thames & Hudson

  Magazines And Trend Reports: As there are an endless array of magazines, both trade and domestic, we recommend that you contact a reliable agent in your area

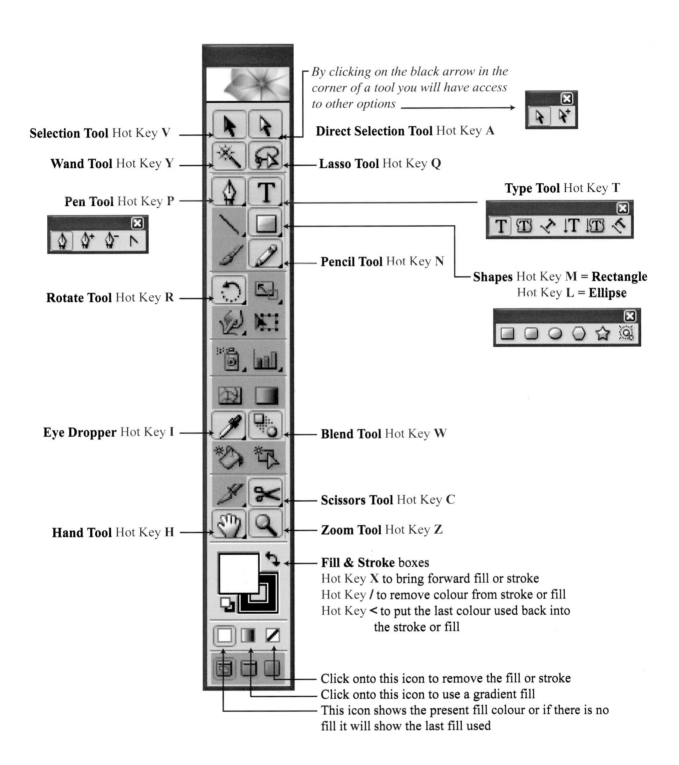

By clicking on the black arrow in the corner of a tool you will have access to other options ————————→

Selection Tool Hot Key **V** ————→ **Direct Selection Tool** Hot Key **A**

Wand Tool Hot Key **Y** ————→ **Lasso Tool** Hot Key **Q**

Pen Tool Hot Key **P** ————→ **Type Tool** Hot Key **T**

Pencil Tool Hot Key **N**

Shapes Hot Key **M** = **Rectangle**
Hot Key **L** = **Ellipse**

Rotate Tool Hot Key **R** ————→

Eye Dropper Hot Key **I** ————→ **Blend Tool** Hot Key **W**

Scissors Tool Hot Key **C**

Hand Tool Hot Key **H** ————→ **Zoom Tool** Hot Key **Z**

Fill & Stroke boxes
Hot Key **X** to bring forward fill or stroke
Hot Key **/** to remove colour from stroke or fill
Hot Key **<** to put the last colour used back into
the stroke or fill

Click onto this icon to remove the fill or stroke
Click onto this icon to use a gradient fill
This icon shows the present fill colour or if there is no
fill it will show the last fill used

THROUGHOUT THE BOOK ALL APPLE MACINTOSH OS COMMANDS WILL BE HIGHLIGHTED IN
BLUE WHERE THEY ARE DIFFERENT TO PC COMMANDS. Please note that the Toolbox commands are the
same for both Apple Macintosh and PC.